KV-602-728

WHERE'S MY F*CKING LATTE?

...AND OTHER STORIES ABOUT BEING AN ASSISTANT IN HOLLYWOOD

MARK YOSHIMOTO NEMCOFF

GLENNEYRE PRESS
Los Angeles, CA

Published by Glenneyre Press 2007
a division of Glenneyre Press, LLC.
www.glenneyrepress.com

ISBN-10: 1477520848
ISBN-13: 978-0-1477520840

Where's My F*cking Latte?
Copyright © 2007 Mark Yoshimoto Nemcoff.

Third Edition

*Real names in this book have been omitted
to protect the identities and jobs
of the sources.*

*This book goes out to assistants everywhere.
Without whom, nothing would ever get done.*

AS FEATURED ON TV'S "ACCESS HOLLYWOOD"

PRAISE FOR:
WHERE'S MY F*CKING LATTE:

I can tell you firsthand that what goes on behind-the-scenes of Hollywood's glittering facade is usually shocking, insane and full of sex offers. Where's My F*cking Latte perfectly captures the abusive and often hysterically unbelievable world of celebs and Tinseltown power-brokers and the culture of excess and entitlement they live in. Two thumbs WAY, WAY UP.

- **Daniella Cracknell,** *Publicist to many of TV's iconic stars from Dick Clark, Howie Mandel, Geraldo Rivera, Mario Lopez to name a few...*

CALL SHEET

WHERE'S MY F*CKING LATTE?

...AND OTHER STORIES ABOUT BEING AN ASSISTANT IN HOLLYWOOD

MARK YOSHIMOTO NEMCOFF

FOREWORD

Every movie and TV star has one. So does every agent and manager. Some producers and studio execs have two or even three.

I'm talking about an assistant.

In Hollywood, your assistant is your gatekeeper, gopher, confidant, and right hand.

Keep in mind most people wipe their ass with their right hand.

Truth is, nobody in Hollywood is treated worse than the assistant. I know this for a fact. For three years I was one myself.

You're thinking it doesn't sound so bad, right?

Imagine an entry-level job most people would kill for.

Imagine the chance to work with some of the entertainment industry's top movers and shakers. Getting up close and seeing every detail of how millionaires do business. Being privy to secrets and tricks of the trade. Making friendships and cultivating relationships with agents, managers, stars and power brokers galore.

Imagine fetching coffee and sandwiches. Picking up dry cleaning. Making travel reservations then changing them twice at the last minute, and being yelled at for not getting an aisle seat. Fetching more coffee. Waiting at your boss' house for the maid service to show up, and making sure they don't poach his stash of weed. Driving to Orange County to pick up

1

special toothpicks from Europe because they're the only ones your boss will use, and he *needs* them. Getting a call at home at four thirty a.m. from London because your boss doesn't like his hotel room, and wants you to phone the front desk to fix it instead of going downstairs and doing it himself.

Then imagine nothing you do is right. Imagine living in fear of being fired every time your boss screws up and blames it on you.

In the eyes of the people who sign your checks, you have no feelings. You are nobody. If you had to go, they'd find another fresh-faced kid to put at your desk before you could snap your fingers. Someone else whose spirit they could break with their whining, egomaniacal tantrums and relentless verbal abuse.

Hell, if Gunga Din had worked as an assistant in Hollywood, how many times would his boss have screamed in his face, "Why are there no poppy seeds on this bagel?"

But you put up with it.

Because you know this is the way in; the inside track to the keys to the kingdom.

Your own Porsche. Your own movies. Your own assistant to yell at.

Along the way you hear things, you see things.

Things you're not supposed to tell anyone. Not a soul.

Secrets.

Dirty little secrets...

☆ ☆ ☆ ☆ ☆

THE GUEST STAR (GS)

We had a really famous GS on our TV show one week, and since I had been a big fan of his for years, I practically begged to get the assignment to drive him.

The first day I picked him up I was a bit nervous and didn't say much, but he was pretty cool and we talked a little bit while I drove him home. I told him what time I'd be picking him up the next morning, then I gave him my cell number just in case something came up.

On the second day we were in the middle of the twenty-five minute drive from his house to our soundstage when he told me, rather urgently, he had to pee. I told him I could stop at a fast food joint nearby, but he was very hesitant to do so. Instead, he spotted the half-full Snapple bottle sitting in my cup holder that had been there for days. He grabbed it, emptied the rest of my peach iced tea out the window, then proceeded to whip out his dick in my car.

"Don't look," he told me. I thought he was just fucking around. I began laughing so hard I was afraid I was going to get us into an accident.

Without spilling a drop, he filled up the bottle. He twisted the cap back on and held it in his lap the rest of the drive. It was such an intensely weird moment, we didn't even talk about it during the rest of the ride.

When we arrived at the lot, I parked by the stage and he slipped his pee-filled bottle back into my cup holder as he was getting out of my car. He thought I didn't notice, but I did.

Later on, I told a buddy of mine, another PA, about what happened. He practically fell down in stitches. He kidded me that I should put the GS's pee up on eBay. It became a running gag, for the rest of the day whenever we saw each other.

"What's the high bid?"

"Last I saw it was twenty bucks."

"I heard it might go to twenty-five."

And so it went, all day long until it was up around eight hundred and fifty bucks in our little joke by the end of the day.

That night, I got pulled off onto another job and someone else drove the GS back to his place. But I guessed that person must have told him something because as I was driving home late from work, I received an angry call from the GS. He started yelling at me that I better take his bottle of pee off of eBay or he was going to hurt me physically and financially. I mean, he was really blowing a gasket. When I finally got a word in edgewise, I tried to explain it was just a joke, and that I never put his bottle up for auction. He told me that when I picked him up in the morning I'd better have the bottle with me to show him I still had it. I told him fine, then hung up before he got all heated up again.

And that's when I realized I was in trouble. I didn't actually have the bottle anymore. I had tossed it out into the trash back at the lot.

I thought about what I was going to tell him. I realized he'd never believe me if I gave him the truth, so I stopped at a 7-Eleven near my apartment and picked up an identical bottle of Snapple Peach Iced Tea and chugged it.

By the time I got home it had done the trick. I took the bottle inside and filled it up to what I was hoping was the same level he had that morning.

The next day, I showed up at the GS's house, and sure enough, the first thing he did was ask me if I had the bottle.

When we got to my car, I pointed to the cup holder and to the bottle I'd put there that morning. He looked at it a moment and I got scared he could somehow tell it wasn't the same bottle, wasn't his pee.

"Fine," he grunted.

It was the last thing he said to me all week.

☆ ☆ ☆ ☆ ☆

THE CASTING DIRECTOR (CAD)

Like a great many jobs in Hollywood, mine was acquired thanks to nepotism. My father had been a well-liked character actor around town, and before his death had asked some of his close friends in the business to watch out for my well-being. When I got out of UCSB, I had a job waiting, thanks to a big-shot CAD, who incidentally was also my godfather. I had concerns my B.A. in Sociology with a minor in Jewish Studies wasn't really going to help me, but my new boss looked me in the eye and said, "Honey, this is Hollywood. Nothing could be more perfect."

I basically came in as the "third assistant," which meant in the office hierarchy I occupied the bottom rung. Aside from answering phones and fetching coffee and lunch, I drew the duty of opening up the dozens of actor headshots and resumes being mailed to us every day. From these, I was instructed to divide them into two groups. One for anything sent to us from an agency or manager, and a slush pile of unsolicited hopefuls trying to get our attention. When there was time, we'd flip through the slushies to weed out the "no chancers." Anyone with crossed or wandering eyes was a "no chancer." To my surprise, I soon learned there were a fairly large number of people with ocular disorders who fancied themselves as the next Brad Pitt or Julia Roberts.

At first, I would feel badly about throwing away these photos someone had spent money on, that someone had loved enough to pin their hopes on and took the time to mail to us. I imagined them sitting in their homes in Silverlake or Idaho waiting for a phone call offering them a chance at their dream, waiting for a call that would never come. Within two weeks, I realized I'd become hardened to the task of "flaw-finder" when I held up a particularly bad one and jokingly asked my office mates if they thought this pop-eyed "no chancer" would be able to see behind himself without even turning his head.

Anyone who eschewed a professionally done headshot for a disposable camera snap or Polaroid was also a "no chancer." People who sent long, pining letters telling us they'd always dreamed of being an actor and if they only got a break, they'd be set. People with bad shrapnel-acne, obviously bad toupees and cheap false teeth. Those who included little "gifts" with their submissions—like the guy who sent us a big t-shirt with his headshot printed on the front, and the mother of four from Las Vegas who included a tin of home-baked Toll House cookies. All of these went into the trash. They were all "no-chancers." One guy sent us photos of himself laying on a slab, made up like a cadaver. In his letter, he tried to explain why he'd be perfect to play some of the corpses on CSI. I threw that one out fast, doubly creeped out that he kind of looked like a guy I had dated once in college.

On occasion we'd get calls from people following up on their submissions. The "no chancers" were as easy to spot as Mike Tyson in a bowl of rice. Unlike the no B.S. demeanor of agents, managers, producers or their assistants, "no chancers" would stammer and sound nervous. You could feel their desperation practically oozing from the phone. In the great Hollywood tradition of *don't call us, we'll call you*, my standard response quickly became, "Everything that comes through the door gets looked at and if we think you're appropriate for something, we'll contact you." The part about not letting the door hit your ass on the way out was never spoken though, at least telepathically, implied.

After receiving the standard brush off from me, one very young-sounding actor began to cry on the phone. Between sobs he told me he'd been trying for five years to get a part and was having no luck getting a break. He asked if I thought he should give up acting altogether. Against my better judgment, I told him he should keep trying as long as he was passionate about it. I asked how old he was. He answered that he was ten.

"Really?" I asked, completely astonished by how mature he'd been.

"Actually, I'm twenty-one," he said, tittering. "See, don't you think I'm a good actor?"

Another group of "no-chancers" my boss wanted nothing to do with were transsexuals. Barely a week would pass without a tranny headshot coming through our mail slot. Though some were extremely gorgeous (making me quite jealous how many of them claimed to fit in a smaller dress size than me), we received our share of she-male photos that were scarier than anything in a Wes Craven movie. One of them, who my office-mate dubbed "Miss Penis," was the spitting image of the lead singer of the Heavy Metal band Whitesnake. To make things worse, Miss Penis had a very pronounced Adam's apple that, possibly due to the lighting in the photo, looked to be as big as a baby's fist.

When I mentioned to one of the other assistants that I'd heard there were other casting agencies in town that specialized in cross-gendered talent, she replied that our boss had been *burned* by a tranny before. Considering my godfather's alleged reputation for occasionally getting a piece of strange every now and then, I decided I was going to remain blissfully ignorant of what she really meant.

Truthfully though, most of the ones who made it past the first cut fared no easier. We'd often have contests to see who could find a headshot of an old woman with the biggest glasses. One of the running jokes around the office would be to pick some headshots from the slush pile as if we were casting the "Kenosha Valley Dinner Theatre Presentation of..." some famous TV show. Though I worked hard on my first attempt, my pass at a cast for *The Dick Van Dyke Show* using all Filipino actors paled in comparison to the first assistant's rendering of the *Brady Bunch* comprised of gangbangers. The picture he chose to represent "Bobby" was so eerily close, gang tats aside, that at first I thought he'd taken the real thing and Photoshopped it.

It was my boss, however, who trumped all of us when he posted his alleged cast of *Three's Company* using the headshots of two morbidly obese women paired with a smiling young man who obviously suffered from a severe case of Down's Syndrome. Once again, he proved beyond a shadow of a doubt why it was his name on the door.

Because my boss came from the old school, he eventually gave nearly every headshot in the slush pile at least a glance before circular filing them.

"You never know when you'll find a gem," he'd say on such an occasion. Because casting is such an optimistic business, we all believed it, too.

In the end, I came to the realization that even though I'd grown up around it, the hustle and bustle of Hollywood wasn't going to be for me. I think my godfather knew it too. When I told him I'd been offered a corporate job working with "civilians," he hugged me and gave me his blessing.

I still speak to him twice a month. Every now and then he'll ask if I want to come down and root through the slush pile for laughs.

Not too long ago, I had a friend at my new job approach me about getting one of her kids into movies. She'd heard me talk about working for my godfather, and wanted to know if I'd pass along her oldest daughter's headshot. I could see the manila envelope in her hand and kept my best poker face as I took it. I told her I'd see what I could do.

Back at home, I sat at my kitchen table, poured myself a glass of wine and opened up my friend's envelope. I was prepared for a big chin, jug ears, even a harelip. What I saw was a perfectly beautiful kid with obviously bad skin underneath a spackle job of foundation. I sipped my wine and slipped the headshot back into the envelope. After thinking about it, I took out a small sheet of paper and wrote: "I hear she's a great kid." I knew it wouldn't stop the crew at my godfather's office from casting her in the next Kenosha Valley

Dinner Theatre rendition of *Petticoat Junction* opposite a pair of pizza-faced hopefuls, but I could at least look myself in the mirror and tell myself I tried.

Though I've been out of the business for a couple of years, I heard something the other day that made me sad. Apparently quite a few people in Hollywood believe computer generated, fully three-dimensional avatars will someday replace actors. So if a director wants a busty blonde all he'll have to do is manipulate a few sliders on a computer screen and, voila, there she'll be, ready for her close-up. Someday human actors, and surely enough, casting directors, will be as obsolete as the telegraph.

But I have to think that even if this happens, even if technology advances to the point this fantasy becomes reality, somewhere there'll be a micro chip called the *Castmaster 3000* analyzing a virtual headshot and computing its own levels of simulated jealousy at whether the CGI tranny it's looking at truly wears a size four.

THE HEAD OF DEVELOPMENT (HOD)

My boss, the HOD, was blessed with an empty house for the upcoming three-day holiday weekend. His wife was taking the kids out of town to visit her parents. A lot of guys I know would take a couple days of temporary bachelorhood to go "alley-catting." Not my boss. He relished the chance to finally catch up on his reading pile. He planned to stay at home with all the scripts he could carry. Just him and the family's hundred–and–ten-pound Burmese Mountain Dog, Max (not his real name).

My weekend, however, was another story. I had an old friend come into town and made it a point to show him all the sights. Also to renew our old boozing rivalry where we'd match each other toe-to-toe, drink-for-drink, all night long; the loser bearing the brunt of months, sometimes years, of merciless ragging, not to mention the mother of all hangovers. As I was soon to find out, my buddy had come to town with his "game face" on. I stood no chance. Though I tried valiantly, I faded fast in the homestretch and had to be carted home in an embarrassing state of unconsciousness.

My phone began ringing at ten Sunday morning, the sound of which made my head feel like it was about to explode into a million pieces. I let it go to my answering machine. The voice broke through. It was my boss. He was in a panic. I picked up the handset, setting off a squeal of feedback that nearly killed me. I tried to understand what he was saying but my brain couldn't process it. The only thing I could understand was that he needed me to come to his house right away. I hung up the phone and sat up too fast. When the room stopped spinning, I realized, without much surprise, that I was still in my clothes from the last night.

My buddy had already split to catch his plane back to Portland, leaving me a note that said: "Better luck next time." I grabbed my car keys, feeling like I was going to be sick. The thought of getting behind the wheel of my car made me pray for death.

Somehow, I made it over to my boss' house in twenty minutes, thankfully due to light Sunday morning traffic. When I pulled into the driveway, he ran out in his bathrobe. I could see he had been crying.

"It's Max," he said, choking the words out.

I followed him into the backyard and my boss pointed. I had to squint. There, underneath the pool's translucent solar cover, at the bottom of the deep end, was a motionless Max.

"What happened?" I blurted. I thought of all the times I had come over to his house and Max had nearly bowled me over, licking my face and happily sniffing my crotch with total innocent abandon. He was as lovable a dog as I'd ever known, and now to my complete and utter horror, he was lying dead at the bottom of the pool.

My boss explained he had been reading on the couch in the family room the night before. Sometime around ten, he had let Max out to do his evening's business.

"I must have fallen asleep," my boss said. "I woke up on the couch around six. The script I never finished was still on my chest." He said that after a short while he began to realize Max wasn't in the house. He first thought Max had gotten out of the yard (something he'd done before) and was running loose in the neighborhood, possibly tearing up someone's flower garden. He told me how he ran up and down the street holding Max's food dish, tapping a spoon against it, making a sound the dog always associated with mealtime. It was only an hour previous that he looked in the backyard and found that Max had drowned.

"He might have been chasing a squirrel." My boss said squirrels sent Max into a complete frenzy. To my horror, I could imagine the hundred-and-ten-pound Max inadvertently making that fatal turn onto the pool cover, only to find out too late it wouldn't hold his weight. I tried to put the rest of the image of him struggling to get out from under it out of my head. Poor dog. I began to sob hysterically.

"We have to get him out of there," my boss said. And right then I realized *we* actually meant *me*.

I looked around to find something to help with the gruesome task at hand. In the corner of the yard I spotted the pool net, the pole already severely bent.

"I already tried that," my boss said. "He's too heavy."

The hollow feeling in my tummy got worse as my boss said the following: "One of us is going to have to go down there and get him."

I stood there, mouth agape, hangover of doom throbbing between my ears, and contemplated the inescapable fact that I had obviously done something very terrible in a previous life to deserve this.

"I'll get you a bathing suit," my boss said. Before I could protest any further, he disappeared into the house.

Moments later, I had changed in the guest room into what I hoped was a clean pair of my boss' swim trunks. I stepped out into the yard, my bare feet feeling the chill of the recently watered lawn as I crossed over to the pool. I looked over at my boss, who was still fully clothed.

"I'd go in, too, but I can't hold my breath underwater for shit," he told me. It sounded like a complete load, but I knew for a fact my boss couldn't swim. The closest he ever came to the deep end was sitting in the attached spa. He handed me a thin nylon rope.

"Tie one end around him and I'll help pull him out from here."

I looked at the pool and a case of full-body goose bumps broke out from head to toe.

"How cold is the water?" I asked, knowing the chance of my boss heating the pool this soon before Memorial Day was zip.

"Cold," he said. "Just try not to think about it."

Try not to think about it? Was he kidding me? At that moment it was *all* I was thinking about.

I contemplated diving in, but thought better of it, realizing the sudden cold would probably put me into instant cardiac arrest. Then there'd be two bodies to recover from the bottom of the pool. Instead, I baby-stepped in. The moment my foot hit the freezing cold water up to my ankle, it felt like a jolt of electricity shooting through my body. By the time I'd gotten in to my knees, I thought I was surely going to throw up. At the crotch level, the amount of discomfort had grown to unspeakable proportions. I squeezed my eyes shut so tightly I thought my eyeballs would shoot out of my ears. Under my breath, I had begun to mumble, "Kill me now."

Realizing I had to get the job done quickly before my muscles cramped up, I knew I had no choice. I took the deepest breath I could muster with my constricting lungs and then dove in.

I gritted my teeth. As I swam down to the bottom of the deep end I could see Max clearly. I didn't want to touch him. I tried to loop the rope around one of his back legs and failed on my first attempt.

My air ran out and I kicked to the surface. Gasping for breath, I swore to get it done my second try, because frankly, I didn't know if I could take much more of this.

With thousands of gallons of water pushing down on me, squeezing my head, I looped the rope around Max's back legs. Immediately I could tell how heavy he was. I tugged the line and the waterlogged dog didn't budge an inch. I surfaced, fantasizing about a warm, fluffy towel, and told my boss to pull. He did, but with little luck.

"You're going to have to go down there and push him," he said. I began to contemplate how difficult it would be to explain to my parents why I had quit my job. Instead, I dove back down.

I had avoided looking at Max's front end during my first two dives down to the bottom. This time it was unavoidable. His still and open-eyed face was staring back at me with a somewhat confused look. I kicked against the back wall of the pool and my fingers sunk into Max's fur like it was floating seaweed. I pushed as hard as I could.

Max moved about half a foot.

I swam up to get more air.

"Keep going! Keep going!" my boss shouted.

We repeated this for twenty minutes, until at long last, we were able to get Max to the shallow end. Once there it took the two of us to pull him out of the pool. A hundred and ten pounds alive, Max now felt like he weighed three times that much.

We laid Max out on the grass and my boss began sobbing again as I stood there shivering so hard, I thought I was going to break something. I looked around, hoping to find that warm fluffy towel. It turned out my boss had forgotten to bring one out. I told him I was going to go in and change. My feet were wet and I was shivering. As I stepped on the linoleum floor outside the guest bathroom, I slipped, landing hard on my ass. I just sat there and wanted to cry.

THE VERY FAMOUS ACTOR (VFA)

We repped a VFA who hadn't had a hit in quite a while, and was considered by many to be on the downslide. Whatever effect this had on his ego was negligible, because he continued his partying like nothing in the world was different. He was known all over Hollywood for it.

He and I had become decently acquainted from having talked on the phone quite a bit and chatting when he came by the office. I'd been a big fan since high school, so telling people I was on a first name basis with him was one of the best perks of the job. One time, after coming by to do lunch with my boss, he told me he was having a BBQ at his place over the weekend. It was a birthday party for one of his pals, and he told me if I wasn't doing anything to come by and bring some friends. Though he didn't say it, I could tell he meant to bring *female* friends. Honestly, I was kind of surprised, so I told him I'd try to make it.

"Great," he said, giving me one of the smiles that had made him a star.

That Friday, my boss asked if I was really going to the party. I'd been looking forward to it all week, practically bursting when I told my mom about the invite. I decided to play it cool with my boss, though. I told him I wasn't sure.

"Just be careful," he said. He told me the VFA and his friends got crazy on the weekends. He reminded me it wouldn't be good for anybody if I let the VFA fuck me. I had to hold back a laugh. The VFA went for silicone-enhanced Playmate types. I knew I was more than a couple of dress sizes out of his league.

I really only had one friend I dared bring to something like this. Someone who I knew would be cool enough no matter what happened. Someone I knew wouldn't complain if she had to take a cab home on the off chance I got lucky. We didn't want to get to the party too early, so she came by my place and we smoked a joint and tore through a bag of Doritos. She had just gotten a job at a cable net and bought herself a new car. This and the fact I knew she could eat as much junk food as she liked and never gain a pound made her my hero. She was utterly fearless.

We rolled into the party to find the VFA's place pretty hopping. He'd bought this house in Hancock Park years ago, and with the exception of a couch, a bedroom set, a dining table and a few big screen TV's, had never bothered to furnish the place. It had become a party pad for him and his close circle of friends, and the wide-open spaces made it perfect for their legendary weekend blowouts. Stacked in the dining room were cases and cases of booze.

After a short while, we found the host. The VFA did something very cool. In front of everybody, he gave me a big hug and greeted me like we'd known each other forever. When I introduced my friend, I totally expected him to hit on her, but he was utterly charming. He told us to make ourselves at home and if anybody started bugging us to let him know, and he'd take care of it. It was like having the world's coolest big brother.

The VFA manned what looked to me like the biggest stainless steel gas grill I had ever seen, cooking up dogs, burgers and chicken for everybody. My friend and I ate, had a couple of drinks, mingled and talked to a lot of people we already knew. More than once, I remarked to my friend how the party wasn't nearly as wild as I'd been led to believe it would be.

Then around nine, the VFA's posse showed up. Five guys, all of them having come up in the business together, and all of them trouble. It was as if someone flipped a switch. Instantly the music got louder, thumped harder, and you could just feel the whole party going into overdrive. The birthday boy was already drunk off his ass.

One of the guys in the posse, a fairly well-known character actor, spotted my friend and came over to talk to her. They'd met before, and he flirted viciously with her without ever once looking at me. When he walked away, my friend confessed something.

"I slept with him once when I first came to town years ago," she told me. My jaw dropped. She shrugged. There had been some crazy days for all of us.

Not too long after that, a big limo pulled up to the house. It was a pretty famous photographer who was well-known for providing "talent" to some of the best parties in town. Tonight was no exception. In tow were a half dozen girls who looked like they had stepped off the pages of Penthouse. Every eyeball, male and female, became glued on this bevy of beauties as they entered the party. Though each red-blooded man there drooled on his shoes as they passed, nobody dared approach. These girls were reserved for the host and his posse.

"You know they're all pros," my friend said.

I was so naive that I thought she meant they were all actresses. My friend told me these girls were all "compensated" for their time by the photographer. Apparently, he used them to get in with the "in crowd." In a town that I'd once heard described as the *NASDAQ of Pussy*, I wasn't surprised one bit.

"Some of them are models and actresses," my friend further explained. In an odd way, I felt better I had been somewhat correct in my first assessment.

As soon as the "talent" arrived, the VFA swooped in to welcome the newcomers to the party. My friend and I retreated to a safe spot on the other side of the pool to watch. We joked to each other that we both felt like Jane Goodall spying on the mating rituals of primates.

It was getting close to eleven and though it was pretty early, my friend and I were ready to call it a night. My friend's old one-night stand came by. He put his arm around both of us. He was slobberingly drunk.

"You guys aren't taking off, are you?"

"We are," my friend said.

"And if you think we're guys, then you're drunker than you think," I added. He was too sloshed to get the joke.

"Aw, come on, stay." He was practically begging. I'd come to know this as the passive-aggressive way actors got things in Hollywood. We were halfway to the door when he pulled out the big guns. He called the VFA over to help him plead his case.

I'd seen the VFA put away a few drinks, but he was as charming as ever. He told us it wasn't even midnight and the party was just getting started. He called someone over with a tray full of shots and insisted we all do one with him. In his own way, he made it seem like it was our idea.

Three drinks later we were still at the party, dancing with guys from the posse and some other hangers on. My friend's old one-night stand had moved on to other prey. I got stuck with the birthday boy. He kept telling me he had met me before but I knew we hadn't. I asked him if he was having a good birthday. He told me he was, but the VFA was upstairs with his presents. It took me a second, but I realized he was talking about the pros the photographer had brought with him.

A couple of drinks later and I found myself out by the side of the house making out with him in the darkness. He had one hand up under my bra and was trying to put my hand on his crotch. He kept asking me to give him a birthday present; one that he would receive orally. After some more pleading, I agreed to a hand job. The problem, however, wasn't my willingness, but the birthday boy's inebriation keeping him from staying hard long enough to complete the act. Mercifully, after about a minute, his cell phone rang. It was the VFA calling to see where he was.

I prayed he wouldn't mention he was with me, or what we had been doing. Thankfully he didn't. He hung up and told me the VFA was flying himself and "the boys" to Aspen. They were leaving in ten minutes. I had a feeling they weren't going alone.

I left him as he zipped up. To my relief, he didn't thank me. He didn't say anything.

A short while later, I found my friend and told her what happened and she burst out laughing so hard I thought she was going to have an embolism. I told her all I wanted was to go home and wash my hand.

We left the party as the VFA, his posse, the photographer and the talent piled into the limo on their way to the waiting G4 warming up on a runway somewhere. I could almost imagine the birthday boy drunkenly asking one of the pros for a present.

Sunday, I nursed a wicked hangover, and Monday I went into the office vowing never to do that kind of thing again. My boss asked me if I had gone to the party and I told him I did but it was no big deal. I told him how gracious a host the VFA was to me.

"I hope you didn't sleep with any of his friends," he said. "You know they all have herpes."

I had been trying to play it cool, but my sudden look of horror must have betrayed me.

"Just kidding," my boss said as he entered his office laughing his ass off.

THE BIG TIME PUBLICIST (BTP)

I worked for a BTP who was a hardcore sports junkie. In our office were scores of photos of him playing tennis with some of his most famous clients, including a pair of Academy Award Winners and a famous late-night talk show host. On weekends he'd surf and play roller hockey down by the beach. Even a few years past forty, he was in superb shape and prided himself on it, always pushing himself harder.

One weekend, he took a pretty bad spill during a game and twisted his back. He was in agony. His doctor put him in a soft brace and restricted his physical activity for at least a month. For health reasons, he resisted a prescription for Vicodin, opting instead for mega-doses of ibuprofen for the discomfort. I heard the story on Sunday and remarked to my girlfriend at the time that even though he was laid up, nothing short of hospitalization would keep him away from the office. I was right.

Though he could still drive, he was now walking with a temporary cane like my eighty-five-year-old grandfather. On Monday morning he called me into his office. He'd always been a very frank person and wasted little time explaining his problem in excruciating detail. Because of his injury, he was having trouble in the bathroom. In particular, he was having quite a difficult time bending his body to wipe himself. My mind rocketed toward the horrific possibility of what I was about to be asked. Not even my recent raise would cover that one.

Instead, he told me he'd spoken to his doctor who'd recommended a "special tool" that had been developed for handicapped people. Basically, it was a stick with a handle on one end and a grippy-device on the other to hold a wad of toilet paper. It was invented to enable extremely obese people to have access to areas they were physically unable to reach. He asked me to find a place that sold them and get one as soon as possible. I asked him if he knew the name of the device. He shook his head and told me to call his doctor and ask.

When I couldn't reach my boss' doctor on the phone, I resorted to the Internet. I Googled "Ass wiping stick," "Butt wiping tool," "Disabled bottom wiping," "Obese rectal hygiene swab" and every combination of short descriptive phrases I could think of. What I mostly found were juvenile Internet discussions of bodily functions, including an entire website dedicated to how people poop. To my utter horror, the site was loaded with dozens of photos.

Thoroughly flummoxed, I had become convinced this device didn't actually exist. I was very hesitant to ask anyone else in the office to help me because of the confidential nature of the matter at hand. To make things worse, it was a regular crazy Monday and the phones were blowing up left and right. My boss was in the middle of negotiating appearances for a hot, new young client and debating the age-old question around here of who got her first, *Dave or Jay?*

As I was holding off the booker from *Kimmel* on one line and a writer from *Marie Claire* on another, my boss hobbled past my desk and asked quietly if I'd had any luck. I listened to the woman from *Marie Claire* jabber in my ear as I shrugged to my boss. He pointed to the phone book. I understood what he was saying.

When I got a breather, I began dialing up medical supply stores around town. Speaking as quietly as I could, I carefully asked if anyone had the "personal wiping stick" I was looking for. The first place I called, a man with an East Indian accent hung up on me. Flipping to the next listing, I tried again, and again. One man tried to sell me a "self cleaning" toilet seat which he described as having a "fairly high powered, built-in bidet." I told him what I was looking for would have to be portable since it would need to be used in more than one location. He continued to tell me it was "easily installable" and came with a warranty.

On the fourth call, I hit pay dirt. The kindly woman on the phone knew the product, but told me it would be a special order. "Three or four days," she told me. I was certain my boss couldn't wait that long. I asked her for the brand name and the manufacturer of the product before lying that I'd have to call back.

Armed with this information, I tried the only other places geographically close to us. Nobody had a Homecraft brand Toilet Tissue Aid in stock. I turned back to my old friend, the Internet.

It took me a couple of minutes to locate a site marketing living-enhancements for morbidly obese. To my surprise, they stocked several different sizes ranging from a folding white plastic wiper for travel to a heavy-duty stainless-steel model that looked like a foot-long surgical clamp. Unsure of what my boss would want, I waited until he got off the phone before discreetly asking him.

"Get both," he told me.

As I was leaving his office, he stopped me.

"Don't have them sent here," he said, meaning the office. "Have them shipped to your apartment." I could tell he wanted to have to avoid the embarrassment of having the UPS guy cart a box of ass-wiping sticks into the workplace. He picked up his phone to make a call. "Overnight delivery," he told me as I left.

As I put in the order, I decided against using the company credit card. The last thing I wanted was someone from Visa calling accounting to make sure we'd actually ordered a butt wiping tool. I decided to use my own card and have my boss reimburse me directly. I looked at the 800 number on the website and thought of all those headset-clad operators taking orders for personal hygiene aids and pressurized, easily-installable, self-cleaning toilet seats. I imagined them huddled in a corner during their breaks saying things like, "Yeah, I had a guy who ordered *two* Homecraft Wipers, the big one and the small one. Here's his address." I decided to just use the online order form instead. I was only hoping they would ship them inside a brown cardboard carton and not in their original packaging. To my great relief, during checkout, I saw an option that offered me a free-of-charge greeting card. I tried to think of what it should say:

Hope everything comes out okay?...

Enjoy?...

Happy trails?...

I decided to leave the message box blank. I did see however, that I had a choice of gift wrap. For a moment, I stopped and thought about this. My phone was ringing. The caller was a client who'd heard about my boss' mishap. As I explained to her about what happened, I looked at the pull down menu on my order form.

Balloons or Flowers.

I listened to the client redirect the conversation to her. As she droned on about how she had fallen a couple of weeks back and thankfully wasn't hurt, I stared at my screen.

Balloons or Flowers? Balloons or Flowers?

Finally, I could see my boss was off his call. I patched the client in to his line. Hanging up my phone it came to me all of a sudden like some kind of great epiphany.

I chose flowers.

☆☆☆☆☆

THE CELEBRITY COUPLE (CC)

I work for the male half of an internationally known CC. My boss keeps Great Danes and because of the high risk these dogs run for torsion and bloat, a lot of kennels in L.A. won't board them. So whenever my boss and his wife leave town together, which is often, their palatial house in Bel Air becomes mine.

I eat their food. I swim in their pool, and though I tell them I use one of the guest rooms, I sometimes sleep in their king size bed. All in trade for taking care of Rocky and Bullwinkle (not their real names). Rocky is the grand old man of the house who loves the Jacuzzi when it isn't turned on. On hot days, you'll find him sitting with his head sticking out to the side, whiling away the hours waiting for mealtime. Bullwinkle, on the other hand is practically a baby. Though barely a year, he still weighs in at about a hundred pounds and due to separation anxiety will start to tear up furniture if he's left alone for even a night.

This is a dog that seems always full of energy. He can chase a tennis ball or pull at his rope bone for hours. What he loves best is when you tug on the other end with him. More than anything, he loves people and he loves to play. Though most of my friends tell me what a great perk this is, I have to admit sometimes it gets to be a real drag. Sometimes I want to be in my little apartment because it's *my* apartment. Sometimes my boss gets on my nerves when he tells me how I have to make sure I *do* this and *do* that when I have to stay at his place because his dogs can't sleep in an empty house.

What makes it better is this girl I have up in San Jose who occasionally flies in for a weekend whenever I have the mansion to myself. Whenever she comes to town, I know it's going to be a good time. She's twenty, has a tight little body and loves to go all night long. She is, without a doubt, a one hundred percent sure thing.

One weekend, my boss and his wife are off to Tahoe, and Melanie (not her real name) comes down to keep me warm. I cook her dinner in my boss' chef's kitchen, we play with the dogs, have some drinks from my boss' bar, and after making sure Rocky's dog bed is fluffed, and Bullwinkle has a rawhide bone to chew on, I take Melanie to bed.

We repair to my boss' bedroom and make very good use of every inch of their California King. We go at it for hours. I know doing it in my boss' bed, with his clothes hanging in his walk-in closet nearby and his cologne on the dresser, is a big aphrodisiac for her. She is insatiable, fucking me in every way imaginable for hours and hours. She is like every porno movie I've ever seen rolled into one.

So the next morning, I am woken up by the sensation of Bullwinkle licking my hand; his way of telling me I've slept past his breakfast. I get up and leave Melanie happily dozing. I go downstairs and feed the dogs, and since I can't ever manage to go back to sleep once I've woken, I decide to go for a jog. Quietly, I slip into some running clothes and do a few loops around the neighborhood. I come back to the house and go upstairs. Laying in the bed, asleep and still naked, is Melanie.

One look at that rocking little hard body of hers though, and I'm getting serious wood. I strip my clothes off and go to her, standing naked by the side of the bed. Even though she's asleep, I brush the head of my rock hard gently against her mouth. What I love about Melanie is that she requires very little prodding. Her eyes flutter open and within seconds she's inhaling me.

I am immediately lost in the moment. I close my eyes, savoring the best blowjob of my entire life. My brain is registering only one single emotion: pleasure. Melanie starts working me like a demon. I can feel her mouth on my shaft. I can feel her sucking on my balls. I can feel her tonguing my ass...

And all of a sudden, a thought comes to me. How come I can feel her in both these places at the same time?

I look around and there's Bullwinkle cleaning my undercarriage; his big brown eyes gazing at me lovingly as he jams his big tongue up my balloon knot.

I jump five feet in the air.

Melanie has no idea what's going on and when I try to explain it to her, she begins laughing so hard that I think she's going to have an embolism.

"Do you think someone *taught* him how to do that?" she asks, giving me pause to think about it for a moment.

A few days later, I was there at my boss' house when he and his wife arrived back home.

"How are my babies?" he asked. Rocky was up on his hind legs slobbering all over his master's beaming face.

I was holding Bullwinkle's collar, thinking about the intimate encounter we shared and whispering in his ear. "Go give daddy a kiss. Go give daddy a kiss."

THE TELEVISION PRODUCTION COMPANY (TPC)

I used to dream of the day I'd have kids.

That was until I got a job working at a TPC and met my boss' son, otherwise known as the Spawn of Hell incarnate.

When I was growing up there were some boys who lived across the street that I wasn't allowed to play with because their mother let them smoke her cigarettes. In my mother's eyes, any parent who would allow that kind of thing were horrible monsters. In contrast, my boss and his young wife made my old neighbors look like the Cleavers.

Tad (not his real name) was six and had been raised at home for all of his young life by his mother and a housekeeper/nanny. As such, he had the interpersonal skills one often sees in dogs who have never been socialized. "Prone to tantrums," as my boss once described him, which was much like saying trailer parks are prone to tornadoes.

My first exposure to "Tad the Bad," as another production assistant had dubbed him, came on a day his mother had pretty much unceremoniously dumped him in our office so she could get a massage. It was then I learned his favorite words were, "Bitch" and "Asshole," as in "You're an asshole" and "You're a bitch." As there seemed to be very little love lost between his parents, I can only imagine where he picked up these choice gems of conversation.

Given how busy my boss was, or at least pretended to be, he would often shut his door leaving Tad to roam the office. This was everyone else's cue to hide under their desks. One time, as I was rushing to make offline dubs to messenger out to the network, Tad got into a box full of Styrofoam packing peanuts. After dumping them all over the dub room floor, Tad the Bad commanded me to pick them up. I told him I'd do it when I was done. To which he told me, "Do it now, asshole, or I'll tell my Dad."

Keep in mind that he was six.

Even so, this was no hollow threat. One time I heard my boss chewing someone out because she'd yelled at Tad to get out of the women's bathroom after he'd run in there screaming "Hey, Bitch! Hey, Bitch!" while she was in one of the stalls.

"You don't yell at a kid!" my boss screamed.

It became apparent this was my boss' mantra for child rearing. He wouldn't allow anyone to correct Tad. Perhaps, I wondered, if it was because if he wasn't able to, then nobody was allowed to try and parent his tiny tyrant. Through all of this, most of us wondered where the nanny was. Someone in the office found out the housekeeper/nanny only worked part-time for my boss now. It gave us shivers to think she was turning down work to spend less time around the little monster.

When school started in the fall and Tad entered the first grade, everyone in the office breathed a sigh of relief. It wasn't long, though, before Tad began showing up in the afternoons, usually the busiest time in the office, as we were in full swing producing several cable network shows. Apparently, even having mornings Tad-free wasn't enough for his mother who would bring him straight from school to our office several days a week to accommodate her busy social calendar, consisting primarily of shopping, waxing and manicures.

That was the same fall that "The Apprentice" debuted on TV, expanding Tad's vocabulary to include the Donald's famous catchphrase. Apparently, one day he brought the family's Mexican housekeeper to tears by chasing her around and yelling, "You're fired!" at her all morning long.

It was obvious Tad was learning something at his new school because not too much later, his new favorite word became "Faggot," as in "You're a faggot," a phrase I heard repeated so many times around the office it made me think he was using it the way Hawaiians use the word "Aloha." Everything was "Faggot" this or "Faggot" that, as in "Faggot Bitch" or "Faggot Asshole" or even the occasional, "You're Fired, Faggot!" as he ran up and down the hallways.

One time, I was out front manning the phones for a bit when Tad's mother brought him in for his usual afternoon burn and pillage. He threw a major tantrum. It was apparent he didn't want her to go, though she wanted to hear none of it. As she was leaving, he shouted: "I hate you, you fucking bitch!" She didn't so much as turn back to acknowledge it.

First grade did little to burn off Tad's relentless energy, as he would explode through the office screaming at the top of his lungs and occasionally launch something from someone's desk, be it a stapler, framed photo, or coffee mug. One time, he threw a TV remote at me, catching me just below my eye, before running away, cackling to himself. I didn't dare tell my boss what he'd done, for fear I'd be yelled at, as well.

Before that, I'd only considered Tad an annoyance; a horrible buzzing insect that flew into your ear from time to time. That day, as I looked at the red mark on my cheekbone in the bathroom mirror, I joined the ranks of people I worked with who wanted to throttle that little bastard within an inch of his life.

Then came the time Tad shit himself.

As he ran from room to room around our cramped office, he carried with him the unholy stink of the package in the back of his pants. What he'd done in there was obvious to anyone with a nostril. As polite as possible, people shooed him from their desks until he ended up hovering near me in the break room while I tried to stuff down a late lunch consisting of a greasy microwave burrito. One whiff of Tad's turd was all it took to rob me of my appetite. I dropped my burrito like it was full of monkey pox.

"Can I have that, faggot?" he asked, pointing to what was left of my lunch.

Yeah, that's going to help matters, I thought. I gave it to him anyway.

At some point, someone braver than I finally knocked on my boss' door to inform him about Tad's situation. He was none-too-pleased to have to interrupt his busy workday to clean up the mess. He later approached me at my desk and angrily asked what I'd given Tad to eat.

I tried explaining, in as gentle terms as I could manage, that what happened in Tad's pants had happened before I gave up my burrito.

"Then why'd you give it to him?" Though it wasn't spoken, the word *idiot* was heavily implied by my boss' tone. I really thought my boss was going to fire me. I didn't sleep at all that night, thinking my job had been done in by the shit of a little shit.

Not too long after that, the running, and very hush-hush, joke around the office became that I had poisoned Tad, to which I received many secretive slaps on the back. This spawned a whole new topic of conversation on how to actually poison the little rat. One of the guys offered to make a batch of pot brownies, to which someone told him why waste some good bud when a juice box injected with a teaspoonful of ipecac would really do the trick. He described, in detail, how he could get it into Tad's hands after first wiping his prints off of the drink box. After that, I began to understand some people were really devoting quite a bit of thought to this.

A few weeks later when Tad puked his guts out in the hallway, I heard it was from eating three packages of peanut butter cups, but I had my doubts. I kept my mouth shut though and nobody, even in secret, claimed responsibility, though there was arguably a short list of suspects.

On another occasion, Tad came in with a black eye. He was so sullen that day he spent the whole afternoon in the empty conference room drawing on a pad and occasionally, on the table. I had heard he'd gotten the shiner from an older kid at school who probably had grown tired of being called a, "Fucking asshole bitch faggot."

One guy who would come in and do voice-overs for us whispered that maybe it was our boss who'd finally done it, even punctuating his half-joking accusation with a swing of his backhand. I had to admit I thought it was possible, until I heard my boss was threatening to sue the school and the attacker's parents. However, any sort of plans involving litigation apparently vanished when, a few days later, Tad the Bad pushed the older kid from behind, which wouldn't have been so terrible if the older kid hadn't been at the top of a small flight of steps at the time.

The week Tad was suspended from the first grade, a few people in the office called in sick. He'd spend mornings at home and, presumably when his mommy got tired of dealing with him, he'd get dumped at the office usually just before lunch. I had some Play-Doh that we'd used on a show some time earlier that I gave to Tad, hoping he'd leave me alone. Later, I found out he stuffed the entire contents of the can into the slot of my boss' office VCR. By this time, I think my boss had become a beaten man since he didn't bother blaming me for it.

A few months later, I applied for a new job working at a post house up in the Valley. During the interview I was asked why I wanted to leave my current job. I spouted the usual B.S. about wanting to move up to something that better utilized my skills and would be more satisfying. It was then I saw the family photo on the interviewer's desk. I asked about his kids. He told me they were off at college now. You can only imagine my sigh of relief.

THE DOCUMENTARY FILM PRODUCER (DFP)

My boss the DFP had a house down in Ensenada and would often go there for a few days to chill out between projects. Oftentimes, he would lend it out to friends and family. He had a younger sister I'd talk to on the phone occasionally, but never met, who was going to school somewhere near Sonoma. She'd been hounding him about borrowing the place for a few days. Because of her life-long reputation as a wild child, he knew she'd just be going down there to party, and would most likely trash the place. Finally, though, for her twenty-sixth birthday, he agreed.

She and her female best friend, who was coming along for the trip, blew into the office on a Thursday morning. They'd been driving all night and had plans to make it to my boss' place in time to take a nap and hit happy hour. There was no doubt they were tweaked to the gills by the way they were bouncing off the walls. My boss took a look at the pair of them.

"You're going down there dressed like that?"

They both wore tiny tops and short shorts that made them look like a pair of Hollywood Boulevard streetwalkers. My boss' sister proudly displayed a belly ring. Her friend had a garden of roses tattooed on the small of her back she apparently delighted in showing off.

"Just be careful," my boss sighed, handing over the keys. I could see the concern on his face. At the time I wasn't sure if it was more for them, his house or the general population of Mexico, who were woefully unaware of the tornado about to sweep down across the border.

"Call me when you get there," my boss told her. She was already out the door.

Over the next three hours, my boss called his sister's cell phone twice. Once to remind her to pick up plenty of bottled water in the U.S., and again an hour later to let her know that American car insurance is no good in Mexico. He told her where she could stop in San Diego to pick up a temporary Mexican policy that would cover her there, stressing how important it was. There'd been plenty of stories of *gringos* who'd get into fender benders outside of U.S. soil, only to be rousted by the *Federales*. He told her to stay out of Tijuana.

Now, I'd been to T.J. a dozen times and most of what I'd seen made me think all the rumors of it being a dangerous town were just chicken-shit American paranoia. I'd stumbled out of *Igunas Ranas* drunk off of my ass with loud disco music pounding in my ears several times after dark without incident. I could see my boss was just imagining his sister stopping at one of the unregulated back street pharmacies in T.J., places you could get anything without a prescription, and loading up on Vicodin and Percoset for the long weekend.

Sure enough, a few hours later, my boss' sister called to say she'd arrived safely. I answered the phone and could hear the blender going in the background. They were wasting very little time. The party had already started.

We were in the midst of planning our next project and things at the office were relatively busy. I was on the phone constantly trying to line up interviews and experts to appear on-camera. My boss was tweaking the script and planning a trip to Chicago. For a few days we heard nothing from Ensenada. I got the feeling my boss was more comfortable not knowing what path of destruction his sister was carving through Mexico.

Wednesday around lunchtime she called; they were leaving and she asked if she was supposed to leave the windows open or shut the house up completely. My boss, hoping to air out the place after whatever had happened there, told her to leave them open, that the caretaker would come by and clean the place up. He made the mistake of asking if she'd left the house intact. She told him not to worry, that he was rich enough to pay for anything she'd broken. The answer drove my boss nuts. When he got off the phone, he ranted to me about it for a half hour. He said this was the last time he was going to let her use the house.

Given travel time and traffic, we expected the two of them to roll into the office sometime around late afternoon. By five, when I was packing up to go home, she still hadn't showed up. I could see my boss was starting to get worried. He'd called her and had gotten no answer. I was going to offer to stay, but my parents were in town and I had dinner reservations. Sensing there was nothing I could really do anyway, my boss told me to go. He figured she was probably waiting out traffic somewhere at happy hour.

A little after eight o'clock, as my parents and I were leaving Cafe Del Rey, my phone rang. It was my boss. He was getting frantic. His sister hadn't showed up at all and he'd called several times and had gotten no answer. He was wondering if he should call the police and report her missing, but didn't know if he had to wait like they do in the movies. My father, a lawyer, told me that after the murder of a twenty-year-old SDU student named Cara Knott in 1985, the waiting period changed. In that case, the San Diego County Sheriff's department wouldn't take a missing person's report for forty-eight hours, then later found her murdered under a bridge. Police were now required to investigate any time someone was thought missing without a waiting period.

I asked my boss if he needed me to come into the office. He told me he'd call the San Diego Police and take care of it.

By morning, she still hadn't shown up or called.

My boss had barely slept at all. He'd waited until morning to phone his ailing mother in Arizona with the news. It was a call he was hoping he wouldn't have to make.

At ten a.m., my boss decided he was going to drive down to Ensenada to look for her. Instead of going into the office, he asked me to wait at his house just in case his sister, or the police tried to contact him. Until that point, I'd lived a pretty sheltered life. I'd never known anyone to go missing. Though I'd only met my boss' sister that one time a few days previous, I'd talked to her on the phone lots of times. My stomach was in knots.

In Mexico, my boss spoke to his caretaker who had seen the two girls leave the house around one p.m. My boss begged the man to please ask around to see if anyone else had seen them. *Gringo turistas* were ten to a peso in this neck of the woods, but my boss was hoping someone would have definitely noticed these two particular girls.

The *Federales* were no help. In Mexico, particularly in the coastal regions where tourists frequent, more than sixteen hundred people a year go missing. My boss called me and told me about his conversation with them, which consisted of him filling out a form and them filing it away without looking too closely at it. He said he got the impression they resented Americans coming down there and telling them they had to drop everything to look for their loved ones. "Dropping everything," my boss explained, "would have required them to put down their coffees and to stop bullshitting in the corner near the television."

By that evening my boss had filled up his sister's voice mailbox with messages. The next day he drove up to T.J. to ask around. Nobody he asked remembered seeing the girls, though most of them said they couldn't be sure given the thousands of Americans who come across, most just for the day.

That night, my boss stayed in San Diego. The police had put out an APB on his sister's car, but that so far had yielded nothing more than the fact they were almost certain it hadn't come back across into the U.S. I got a call the next morning asking me to look up the names of private investigators.

After making a few calls, I found someone who claimed to specialize in looking for missing Americans. My boss told me the guy was a stocky little Mexican fellow who intimated he had a lot of connections back across the border. My boss paid him a thousand dollar retainer in cash.

My boss asked me to go to his house and find a photo of his sister to scan and e-mail to the P.I. He knew he didn't have a photo of her best friend. Immediately, we both realized we'd totally forgotten about the other person who, for all we knew, was missing as well.

The problem was we had no leads on how to track down the best friend. We had her first name but nothing more than that. I tried my boss' sister's home number and got an answering machine. I called the place where she worked and was, at first, treated suspiciously until I was able to convince someone that everything I was telling them was the truth. The best friend didn't work there but the manager was able to track down someone who they thought would know her identity. Several calls later, I finally talked to someone who gave me the best friend's first and last name, and the town where she lived.

I got the best friend's number from directory assistance. When someone picked up her phone, my heart leapt. However, it turned out only to be the best friend's boyfriend. He'd been frantic, too, not knowing what had happened. As I tried to explain everything I knew, he burst into tears over the phone. I hung up and realized I had forgotten to ask him to get me a photo. I had to call him back moments later.

My boss spent another day prowling around T.J.; again, he found nothing. He came back to L.A. the next day. He'd been calling all of his friends asking to see if they knew of anyone who might know someone in Mexico who could find out if something had happened to his sister. He arrived back at home looking as if he hadn't slept in days. I was guessing he hadn't.

A week passed, and still no sign of the sister and her best friend. The San Diego Sheriff's department hadn't gotten any further and though the P.I. was checking in every other day with a status report, he'd found nothing so far. After every time the P.I. would call, I'd have the unpleasant task of calling the best friend's boyfriend up in Sonoma. After the first time,

I started to hope I'd only get an answering machine instead of having to talk to him. One time, he mentioned how her parents told him she'd disappeared for a week during high school. She'd followed some band across the country to see them play at Red Rocks outside of Colorado.

I wanted to tell him this wasn't high school and that Mexico wasn't Colorado.

Two weeks later, the P.I. called. The sister's Toyota had been found in T.J. The car had been recently driven, but there were no indications she'd been in it, nor were there any of her possessions in the trunk. Whomever had the car had dumped it. Though it seemed like a pretty big clue, the P.I. told my boss he was afraid it might not lead to much more. The *Federales* could fingerprint the car, but lacked the resources and kind of national fingerprint database for criminals the U.S. had.

A few days later, the P.I. called again. He'd been showing the girls' pictures around and found someone who remembered seeing them on the Wednesday they disappeared. The eyewitness, a club bouncer, remembered the girls were very drunk and were in the company of a couple of men he was certain were Honduran. He remembered the best friend because, on the way out, she lifted her shirt and flashed him. The P.I. had questioned a bar maid at the club who confirmed the girls were with two men she claimed she'd never seen before.

The P.I. warned my boss what he was about to tell him was very unpleasant. He said it was known in certain circles that T.J. was a hotbed of white slavery abductions. If what the club bouncer told him was true, he was afraid this was a definite possibility.

Through one of my boss' friends, we contacted someone at the FBI's San Diego office. The agent confirmed what the P.I. had said about the white slavery trade in Mexico. Such women were kidnapped and shipped off in the dead of night to part of Central America. The cartels that specialized in this, he explained, were based in Honduras. From there, the girls would be beaten, raped repeatedly and shipped off to any part of the world where sex slaves were bought or sold. Young blonde, American women fetched top dollar in places like the Middle East and Asia. Most of the women survived only a few years and were often kept drugged. My boss said it would be impossible to make someone disappear entirely. Grimly, the FBI agent told him those who would try to escape or those who got too old were often taken out to sea and thrown into deep water while chained to cinderblocks, shot and buried in the desert or dismembered while alive and fed to wild dogs. They were killed and thrown away like garbage, their bodies never to be found, their fates never discovered by anyone.

My boss was shaken. He called the P.I and asked him to keep looking. The P.I. asked him to send him another retainer.

The American authorities in San Diego never found anything and my boss only received spotty word concerning the results of the *Federales'* investigation. During one phone call, they denied ever even finding his sister's car. That was a few years ago and nobody has heard from his sister or her best friend since.

Anyone with information related to the disappearances of any Americans in Mexico is asked to contact the FBI's San Diego Field Office at (858) 565-1255.

THE JUNIOR AGENCY PARTNER (JAP)

Compared to the most flaming asshole you've ever known, my boss, the JAP, was the molten hot core of the sun. Sometime during my first couple of weeks working his desk, the topic of Asian movies came up. As I was mentioning my disdain for a particular director's work, I regrettably started my sentence with the words, "Call me picky, but..." Regrettably, because from that point forward he started calling me by new office nickname:

Picky Butt.

"You don't have to call me that," I said, trying to appear to be half-joking.

"But *you* told me to. You said, 'call me *picky, but*'." His shit-eating grin told me I'd never lose this albatross as long as I was drawing breath.

"Hey, Picky Butt, get in here!" he'd page from his office, sometimes doing it when others were within earshot of my desk. Luckily, I never saw anyone laughing at me. I never saw it because they at least had the decency to do it behind my back. Over drinks one night, one of them informed me my boss had also given my predecessor a nickname. I shuddered when I heard it, and woe was me the day I considered myself lucky I hadn't been the one dubbed, "Fucktard."

Nonetheless, it never failed that anytime I gently couched the subject of my office moniker, he'd take pains to use it even more. One afternoon, we were rolling calls when I managed to reach a fairly famous client on set, and I overheard my boss say, "Give Picky Butt the name of your hotel and he'll overnight some scripts to you."

I could tell the client was confused, probably thinking he'd heard wrong, or that my boss had replaced me with some foreign intern. To my embarrassment, I had to quickly explain it was my nickname. That moment will stick with me forever since it's hard to forget the first time a Golden Globe winner snickers at you.

Though I wanted like hell to get another job, anywhere (even working at *Hot Dog on a Stick* would have been less humiliating), I knew all I had to do was hang in there for at least a full year and I'd have made enough connections to land on my feet elsewhere. I had ten more months to go. It was like looking forward to a prison sentence. A close friend referred to it as my own personal *Bataan Death March*.

Any hopes I had the nickname would fade over time were dashed when my boss' protégé, a wise cracking junior asshole of an agent, picked up on it and began to call me that, too. That Christmas, typed into the memo line of my bonus check was the message, "Way to go, Picky Butt." It was the first time I ever deposited a check by ATM instead of bringing it to the cashier window.

One time, my boss was busy trying to close a fairly big packaging deal that basically came down to the witching hour. The network had been pulling the reins on a mostly unfavorable holding deal with an actor they wanted to work with, but couldn't find a project to plug him into. The actor, who had come off a hit series two years earlier, was frustrated at their attempts to get him involved in what appeared to be a carbon copy of his previous big role. My boss repeatedly tried to tell him that repetition is all network suit monkeys knew, that the best and brightest Ivy League grads go to work in politics or Wall Street. Those who graduate in the middle or bottom of their classes come to Hollywood to screw things up for the rest of us. The client made an ultimatum—find him an Emmy-worthy one-hour to top-line or he was going to bolt.

With millions of dollars (and a commission that dwarfed what my father, the High School Calculus teacher, would earn in his lifetime) at stake, we all went into overdrive to make our client happy. My boss' protégé hunted down the script and yet another agent scared up a top-flight director who'd helmed a fairly big summer movie the previous year. With two weeks to go before the actor's holding deal expired, all the parts were in place.

But the network was balking on the choice of director. They'd worked with the guy before and weren't happy with the results. They were insisting on another director they also had a holding deal with, someone we didn't represent and my boss hated. To boot, someone at the network wanted the show's female lead replaced with an actress who had been in so many failed pilots she'd become known around town as the "Kiss of Death."

With literally a day before the deal was to expire, we were holed up in my boss' office, Chinese food and *Nate and Al's* take-out containers littering the place. My boss had seven people on conference call, including the network's president and vice president of drama development, the senior V.P. of business affairs, our star actor and his hard-edged and very vocal manager. The network was finally warming to the idea of a short list of replacement directors we represented, as well. As I sat there next to him, my boss said, out loud into the speakerphone:

"I'll have Picky Butt fax that over right now."

He then turned to me and yelled: "Hey Picky Butt, get off your ass and send these good people the list! Chop, chop!"

As I stood there at the fax machine, I wondered if I'd end up like one of those old actors who have to put their nickname in quotes around their real name so people would later remember who they were.

Two weeks later, I was sending out my resume. A development job had opened up that I wanted. I interviewed twice and didn't get it. I stuck to my guns. A month after that, a friend recommended me to someone at the production arm of Mike Ovitz's new company. I lied to my boss saying I had a doctor's appointment so I could make the interview. The gig was very hands-on. I played it as cool as ice.

Two days later, I was offered the job.

That night, I went home and typed up my resignation letter. As luck would have it, my boss was out of the office most of the next day trying to close another deal. I waited until seven and went into his office. He was back and now stuck on a call with his wife, yelling about something. I held out the envelope and he waved it over impatiently. I handed it to him and left.

No sooner had I pulled out of the parking garage at the office, when my cell phone beeped telling me I had a voice message. My boss had apparently opened up the envelope after I'd left and tried to phone me as I was in the elevator. I never heard it ring.

He sounded enraged. He yelled that I was backstabbing the guy who gave me a break in this business. He sounded as if he was practically frothing at the mouth, eager to tear me a new one. It ended curtly with him yelling, "You better call me, fuckface!"

My hands were shaking. As I hit speed dial for his direct line, my heart pounded like a rabbit. I'd been waiting for this a long time.

He answered on the second ring.

I took a deep breath. "Hello Fuckface," I said, grinning from ear to ear.

THE DIRECTOR WHO WAS HOT ONCE
(DRWHO)

I'd been on the job with a NYC commercial production company for two days when I heard the story about the DRWHO who was coming in to see my boss. Basically, the DRWHO was crawling back looking for work, having burned his bridges on the way out the door when he'd been offered a two-picture deal with Fox. Both films had been miserable disasters, which led to him being tagged as a failure. In essence, his license to make movies in Hollywood had been revoked for the time being. He'd come back to the Big Apple with his tail between his legs.

I'd never met the guy before, but when he came in it was like a tornado had entered the building. He strolled in like a cowboy and grinned at everyone from behind large sunglasses, which I was told rarely, if ever, came off. You didn't have to be near him to feel his presence in the building. Even as I was being introduced to him, several other people from the company came out to say hi. The DRWHO, I soon found out, was a serious backslapper. He whacked one guy so hard, I thought he'd broken the guy's collarbone. Honestly, from the moment I saw the DRWHO, he kind of scared me.

The meeting between the DRWHO and my boss went on behind closed doors for nearly an hour. When it was over, the two of them shook hands and laughed like old brothers who'd just been reunited. As my boss walked the DRWHO out, I overheard one guy behind me tell someone else, "Guess who sold his soul to come back?"

That day the DRWHO had been the topic of gossip everywhere in the office. In one conversation, I learned in the last year the DRWHO had been in rehab and had knocked up, then married, an actress out West who subsequently gave birth to a daughter with Cerebral Palsy. Speculation had been the kid's medical bills had run through the DRWHO's savings, prompting his return home on his hands and knees.

"Last time he was here, people would crawl under their desks when he came in," one editor told me. It was said the DRWHO had apparently mellowed a bit out in L.A. It was also said he'd gotten a bit fatter, too.

Not too soon afterwards, the DRWHO began working on a new commercial for us and was a presence around the office on a daily basis as preproduction started. (Ad agency name omitted) had dreamed up a really quirky concept their soft drink manufacturer client was in love with. At first, things seemed okay, and I'd begun to believe what I'd heard about the DRWHO mellowing.

Until he threw the salad.

The entire team was having a meeting in the conference room and I'd been sent out to fetch the food order from the deli around the corner and had tried my best to set everyone's lunch in front of them without disturbing anything. I'd given the DRWHO his order first since it was at the top of the bag. Before I'd gotten around the table, he interrupted someone in mid-sentence by picking up his container and throwing it at me.

"What the fuck is this garbage?" He was so mad he was spitting.

The DRWHO had ordered a grilled salmon Caesar salad. I was now wearing most of it.

"I ordered a chef's salad!" he screamed at me. I was too stunned to even respond. The room was silent. My boss, whose feathers I've never seen ruffled, pulled me out of the room.

"What the hell just happened in there?" my boss asked me. I could see he was pissed.

In the hallway, I explained how I remembered taking the order down. One of the assistant producers had ordered the grilled salmon Caesar and the DRWHO had said: "Sounds good, make that two." My boss hadn't been in the room, so he had to take my word for it.

"Go get yourself cleaned up," he said, picking lettuce out of my hair. He told me I'd better get the DRWHO a chef's salad.

Twenty minutes later, now wearing an old musty t-shirt from a box down in the prop closet, I came back with a chef's salad. I placed it, gently, in front of the DRWHO who didn't say a word to me.

By this time, word of the incident had spread across our small office like some post-pubescent version of "whisper down the lane." The receptionist asked if it was true the DRWHO threw a hot cup of coffee at me.

"Not yet," I answered.

I spent the rest of the day logging tapes, a chore I hated, but one that didn't require me to duck any flying vegetables. At one point, after visiting the men's room, I came out to find the DRWHO standing in the hallway, yelling into his cell phone: "Well, if you hadn't done so much fucking blow back in the nineties, maybe we wouldn't have had that fucking flipper baby!"

At that moment, I wished I were anyplace else other than standing in that corridor. I momentarily thought about ducking back into the men's room and hiding out there. Before I could make my move, the DRWHO turned and saw me. I just kept my eyes down to the floor and passed him as quickly as possible. I retreated to the dub room and realized the person he'd been talking to on the phone was his wife.

About a half hour before I was about to leave, I was paged to come down to the front desk. Waiting for me there, alongside my boss, was the DRWHO. I nearly froze in my tracks.

"I need you to carry this box of tapes to (DRWHO's name deleted)'s car," my boss told me. "He's parked two blocks up."

It was actually more like five blocks to the garage where the DRWHO had parked. The entire walk over there, he didn't say a word to me, and instead spent the entire time yelling at his wife over the phone. Even as we were waiting to cross Twenty Fourth Street at Avenue of the Americas, he yelled at her so loudly that everyone else waiting at the corner with us could hear the names he was calling her.

"You rotten bitch, I should have you fucking killed," he screamed once, prompting one haughty-looking businesswoman to shoot *me* a dirty look because I was standing next to him.

Finally, we got to the garage and while we were waiting for them to bring his car down, he got off the phone and turned to me.

"Sorry about the salad, kid."

I mumbled something in return, possibly. "Don't worry about it." Mostly, I wanted his car to come as quickly as possible so he'd be gone.

"You should have ducked," he added.

"I'll remember that next time."

Though I couldn't see behind his giant sunglasses, I could tell by the way his eyebrows bent like a V that his eyes had narrowed.

"Hey," he said, his tone sharpening. "Nobody likes a wiseass."

After what seemed like forever, his Vette came down the ramp. He popped the back and I put the box of tapes in. As I turned, he was standing right there; we were nearly face-to-face.

"Here," he said, pressing something into my hand. "To get your shirt cleaned." He got in his Vette and roared away.

I looked down into my hand. He'd given me a dollar.

THE REALITY SHOW PRODUCER (RSP)

When I was seventeen, I was a singer with starry eyes towards the heavens of show business. At that time, my voice teacher had been unsuccessfully trying to push me into entering beauty, er, I mean *scholarship* pageants on the state and national level. One year, through some well-placed connections of hers, she scored some primo tickets for her and I to see the crowning of a certain beauty queen in a certain East Coast city by the sea. While we were driving down there, she took a piece of paper from her purse and handed it to me. She grinned. On the page were the names of ten contestants.

"The network's list of the girls they want in the finals," she explained. "I got it last night."

I couldn't believe it. I told her I heard they didn't decide the finalists until moments before show time. She laughed.

"You have a lot to learn about the way show business works, sweetie."

I refused to believe it. I was certain she was wrong—until until they announced those same top ten finalists, the ones from my voice teacher's list, right there on live TV.

I'm not certain if that was the day I decided to give up being a professional singer or if that was just the day the dream began to die. I didn't want to be at other people's mercy. I wanted to be one of the people making the decisions. Decisions that would secretly influence how people perceive the world. My father told me to go to D.C.; instead I went to Hollywood.

And when I told this story at my first job interview, I was hired on the spot to be the assistant to an RSP.

I think by now, people, in general, realize most TV reality programs use casting agencies to find contestants. At least such was the case for our show. Ours was your standard "put a bunch of strangers in a house" kind of fare, but my boss, the show's creator, wanted something more than we'd seen before.

He wanted freaks.

Not of the sideshow variety. There was already something in development that would pair ordinary folks with obvious weirdos. We were looking for people who my boss called *monkey wrenches*—jerks we were certain would make it very painful going for the other folks in the house.

This, of course, is reality show manna.

Our list of do's and don'ts from the network included the double-underlined directive: *no felons*. My boss made it clear to us that, by legal definition, a felon is someone who has been *convicted*.

"What about misdemeanors?" I asked.

"That's okay," he said. In most states you can get a misdemeanor for running a stop sign or throwing gum on the sidewalk.

What I'd later discover during our first phase of casting is you can also get one in some states for urinating in a department store changing room, shooting cats with a pellet gun, and threatening to throw your wife out the window of a ten-story apartment building. One of my co-workers dubbed this phase of production the "trailer park crawl.."

When breakdowns are sent to casting agencies, they are fairly specific. Ours had two stipulations: nobody who's ever been cast in anything before, and they had to be a troublemaker.

What we initially got were "troublemaker types." One guy, whose headshot made him look like a surfer model, was given to us because we were told he liked to run with a "rough crowd." One look at this chiseled guy's face and I began to think the agent meant the rough crowd that hangs out at the Barney's warehouse sale.

Luckily, through one of the small casting agencies that handle "offbeat" types, we received some packages my boss liked. I got on the phone and arranged for a casting call.

Friday came and our lobby began to look like a cross between the waiting area at a free clinic and the holding pen at county. One guy with tattoos up and down his arms and shocking red hair, whose headshot listed him as "Spyder," kept asking to use the bathroom over and over. One of my co-workers asked if I thought the guy was shooting up in our toilet. I told her if she wanted to go find out for herself, be my guest. She went back to her desk. I surveyed the room and wondered what other freaks we'd be meeting today.

When we finally got Spyder into the room to meet my boss the real truth about him came out. He was a real estate agent from Redondo. The most trouble he'd ever gotten into was the time he and a friend were caught smoking a cigarette in Hebrew school. As he left my boss scribbled the word "poser" on the back of Spyder's headshot.

Such was the truth for nearly everyone else we met that day. One woman told us she was a troublemaker because she never played by the rules. When we asked if she'd be able to take five weeks off to do the show she said she'd have to check with her boss first.

Not everyone was a complete poser though. One guy came into the room and everything about him just reeked of attitude. He even kind of slouched in the chair like we were annoying him. When we started rolling video and asking him about himself, he squinted at us like a gunfighter sizing up his opponent. As the questions started, it became clear this guy had a short fuse and little tolerance for certain minorities. I could tell my boss thought he'd found our monkey wrench.

We'd hired a firm to do our background checks. We ran this guy through and it didn't take long to find out what we needed to find out.

"Your guy's got a record," the investigator told me.

I took down the particulars and went to my boss. I waited until he was off the phone with his wife.

"Arrested in Oklahoma three years ago for sodomy," I told him.

My boss groaned. Even though the charges had been later dropped, it would be a matter of time before someone picked up on it.

"Damn, I thought he was our Ace in the hole," my boss said.

"So did the cops in Oklahoma," I joked. My boss didn't think it was funny.

All in all, we had about a dozen guys on our short list for the role of monkey wrench. Background checks knocked half of them out of the box right away. Five of them were deadbeat dads. One woman had beaten up her elderly grandmother.

We took six candidates to the network for their approval. As is always the case, network guys like to spray on the hydrant as much as possible. After watching our casting videotapes, they tossed four right away. They hated the last two and asked that we try to find some others they could look at. My boss was furious. He felt all the good sociopaths already had work in Hollywood and we were lucky to find the two we had originally picked. The network uttered the three words all of us feared.

Open casting call.

I called to place several ads in alternative weekly newspapers in major markets. *New TV reality show looking for people with serious attitude. Must be 18.*

We asked for videotape, and a recent photo. Within one week, our post office box was jammed with submissions. It became my job to screen them all.

One woman did nothing but scream at the camera. Two brothers sent us a backyard wrestling tape consisting of them beating the crap out of each other while taking turns mugging to the camera. In another tape there was an old guy in a leather jacket who tried to impress us by sitting on his Harley and punctuating everything he said with a rev of his engine.

One guy sent a homemade porno tape in which he had

sex with a woman in a ski mask.

Another woman, who sat in front of a Nazi flag and claimed to be a white supremacist, told about how it had always been her dream to come to Hollywood and be on TV. She went on to say she felt the Jews who run the entertainment industry were the "kind and good Jews.."

"This woman's never been to my temple the Saturday after Oscar Nominations are announced," my boss joked.

"These are all terrible," I told my boss, looking at the pile of tapes we'd gotten. Shows you what little I knew.

My boss grinned. "Send 'em to the network," he said.

At first, I didn't have an idea why he said not to bother with background checks, but the day the network called back about what we'd sent them, I understood fully.

"They want us to pick one of our two original candidates," my boss told me after getting off the phone. "If they hate what you have, give them something they'll hate even more," he explained. It was something his mentor, an older TV producer, had taught him years ago.

"He was definitely one of the good and kind Jews," my boss said. I laughed for a moment, taking a breather before answering the phone and getting ready to put out yet another fire.

THE LITERARY MANAGER (LMAN)

My boss, a pretty big LMAN, had just bought a brand new black on black Porsche Carrera 4. One of the cool perks of my job was getting to drive it from time to time. If he was out of town and needed it tuned, I'd get to take it to the dealer and pick it up. Lucky for me the dealership he liked to use was way on the west side, and his house was in the Valley. That meant a trip down the 405 where I would get to drive like a demon. I can't explain how fast the car could go other than saying that when you put the pedal to the metal, it felt like you were a bullet being fired from a gun.

One time, I picked up the Porsche a couple of days before my boss was to return home from a trip back east. All of my friends had heard me talking about the car and were always prodding me to bring it by. Like a fool, I finally crumbled to the peer pressure.

My roommate was an actor who had just come into town, so he was home in the afternoons. I thought I'd swing by and surprise him with a ride in my boss' baby. When he saw the car pull up, he ran out, half-dressed. I could see his jaw hit the ground. He didn't even own a car. I don't think he'd ever even seen so much money in one place at one time before.

"Get in," I told him.

I backed out of the driveway, careful to avoid hitting the trashcans on the curb. As I dropped from reverse into neutral, my roommate just grinned at me and said those fateful words.

"Hit it!"

And I did, spinning the wheels as the car rocketed forward from a standing start. Within moments the speedo was shooting upwards. I dropped it into second gear, then third. In mere seconds we were already doing sixty. As my roommate let out a big cowboy whoop, I felt so proud of the fact that, for that moment, the car was mine. My mind became fixated on the day I'd be able to buy a car like this for myself. What I didn't realize was that in a few moments, I'd instead own a part of it.

Thanks to a speed bump.

The very same one I'd driven over every day living on this street. The one they had put in to keep dumbasses like me from doing what I was doing right now. The Porsche hit the six-inch tall bump doing close to seventy. The front end responded beautifully. However, I could tell by the loud crunch as the rear end came over the bump that I had fucked up royally.

I pulled over and my roommate peered under the car. "I don't think it's too bad," he said. My heart hoped for the best. My hands were shaking. All I wanted was to get the car back to my boss' house and go get a drink.

When I pulled away from the curb, I knew something was very wrong. The engine, which normally sounded like a symphony, bleated angrily. I closed my eyes and hoped that as I drove further, it would go away.

It didn't.

Finally, as I was halfway to the Valley, I knew I had to take the car back to the dealer. I drove the rest of the way with white knuckles, gripping the wheel like my life depended on it.

At the shop, I tried to explain what had happened. Trying to make it seem like somehow bottoming out on a speed bump was an accident. The service manager took one look and gave me the bad news. The muffler was trashed.

And the worse news: it wasn't going to be covered under warranty.

My voice trembling, I asked how much it was going to cost to fix it. The manager looked me straight in the eye.

"About eight hundred dollars," he said. "Plus tax."

Eight hundred was just a bit more than two weeks of take-home pay for me. I thought of my near-empty bank account. I thought of the thirty-two inch TV set I had just bought that was about the same price.

"Okay," I told him. What choice did I have?

"Won't be done until tomorrow," he told me.

Great, I thought to myself. To add insult to injury, I was going to have to take a twenty-dollar cab ride home and another one back. These, I wouldn't be able to expense.

The next day, my boss called from New York.

"How's the car?" he asked. My throat nearly closed up on me, but somehow I managed to tell him the dealer had to order a part and I was going to pick it up today. He grumbled, annoyed, by what I couldn't imagine since it wasn't going to make a difference. He was supposed to be out of town until Friday anyway.

"Change of plans," he said. "I'm coming back today."

My heart sank. After he hung up, I frantically dialed the dealer, praying the car was done.

"Sometime after two," I was told. The car would be done then. That would give me several hours to get it back up to the Valley. I watched the clock all morning and when lunchtime came, I couldn't eat. It was for the best, I couldn't afford it now anyway.

Finally, I went to pick up the car. The cab ride to the dealership was excruciating. I kept trying to convince myself that losing my job would cost me a lot more than eight hundred bucks. As I signed the credit card slip, I could see the final bill came to fifty-six bucks over that. I took the keys and was about to drive home, broke, when the service manager said he wanted to show me something.

At the car he pointed out to me an inch-long white scratch on the very bottom of the rear bumper. A scratch I had put there when the car bottomed out. I hadn't noticed it before, but now with it pointed out to me it stood out on the black of the car like a sore thumb.

"We can't buff this out," he explained, because of the material the bumper was made out of. "We'd have to replace the panel." It didn't matter at that point how much it would cost to make my boss' car whole again. I was tap-city. I couldn't do it.

I drove all the way back to my boss' house like someone's grandma, never getting the car above fifty miles an hour. I thought of the million and one ways I could try to explain the scratch to my boss. It was tiny. Maybe he wouldn't notice. It was on the underside of the bumper anyway.

I couldn't take the chance. I had an idea. I backed the car into my boss' driveway and made sure nobody was watching. I took a black Sharpie from my briefcase, laid on my back on the ground, and carefully touched up the small white scratch. I closed my eyes and prayed it was good enough.

That night my boss came home, his plane landing at LAX, as I was sitting in a bar on Ventura Boulevard getting drunk.

And my boss never noticed the difference.

THE SHOW RUNNER (SR)

I had been a staff writer briefly; having gotten the job after the back nine pickup of a network sitcom that subsequently got cancelled after one season. Times were tough, and shows were trimming staff to save a few bucks. My agent couldn't get me in anywhere, so after a year of sitting on the sidelines, I swallowed my pride and took a job as a writer's assistant on a quirky cable sitcom. My hope was that I could somehow fast track myself into a promotion onto the staff by making it apparent to the SR how sharp I was.

Being a writer's assistant meant a lot of crud work. Photocopying, more photocopying and even more photocopying. My social life was nowhere, but I felt like I at least had gotten to second base with the office Xerox machine. I'd grab sodas and granola bars or paper cups full of pretzels for the writers if they asked. Everyone who would listen knew my past and my ambitions, and I even felt like the SR was pulling for me.

The only part of the job I liked was being in the room. There was one other writer's assistant and we traded off this duty, each of us doing a couple of hours at a stretch. In the room, I manned the one computer in the corner where I'd take notes and make on-the-fly changes to the script they were working on at the time. Everything I did was output from the computer and projected onto a large screen for everyone in the room to see.

Over time I'd earned enough respect from the staff to feel comfortable to throw out an idea or two when everyone was spit-balling jokes or plot. I knew this was a privilege so I only opened my mouth when I had something to say. On one occasion a punch line I'd come up with on the fly made it into the production draft whole cloth. Even though another writer was credited for the script, I really felt a twinge of pride when my line got a huge reaction during taping.

The whole time, I never took my eye off of the prize. The show was on the bubble for a back nine pickup. That meant they'd have a script or two open for freelancers. I waited until my relationship with the SR was strong enough to ask about being considered if and when something became available. I'll never forget the response.

"Don't worry," she told me. "You won't be forgotten."

To me, this meant I was in like Flynn. A freelance script this season could mean the inside track for a staff position next year. I could finally claw my way out of the copy room.

The news came the week before Halloween. The first four episodes had done well enough to warrant a pickup. When I heard, I forced myself to contain my joy. I stepped out of our soundstage and silently pumped my fist in the air before regaining my composure.

The next few weeks were agony. Every time I had a couple of seconds alone with the SR, I was hoping to get word of the assignment I coveted. I wanted to ask a hundred times, but kept my cool. She had so many fires to put out on any given day, I knew I was very low on her list of concerns. Besides, having been in this situation before, I was pretty certain I'd have to wait until they broke stories for the back nine before I was given my shot.

We crept closer to the New Year and the staff had begun laying out ideas for episodes fourteen, fifteen and sixteen. I felt like it couldn't wait any longer. I lingered around the SR's office one morning around the time I knew she'd show up. Again, I put forth my enthusiasm to get into the game.

"Don't worry," she told me again. "We won't forget about you."

I was hoping for something a bit more specific, something bordering on a concrete promise. When I realized that wasn't coming, I just kept my smile and thanked her.

As stories continued to break, all I could think of was getting my shot. I would take home writer's drafts and study them for places I could interject a comment or joke suggestion. Anything that would make me look smart, funny and ready for prime time.

One night, as I was reading, something caught my eye. I knew it was wrong and I immediately went to my computer to confirm my suspicions. I did some quick research and armed myself with all the info I'd need.

The next day I timed it perfectly to be in the room when that part of the script came up. In it, one of the characters talks about being like the Titanic and laments that it never had a sister ship. The line wasn't supposed to be funny, but poignant. Nobody spoke up, so I did.

"The Titanic actually had two sister ships," I pointed out. "The *Olympic* and the *Britannic*. Both of which also sunk."

Everyone was silent. With this fact in hand, the line in the script didn't work. Someone suggested using the Hindenburg, but that just wasn't funny. My boss was flustered.

"Well, nobody really knows about it," she finally said. "We'll just keep the line."

As we moved on, I detected the tiniest hint of a dirty look from her. I realized immediately what I had done and my heart sunk.

I'd screwed the pooch.

I thought about apologizing, but realized I'd only be making things worse. Instead, I avoided my boss as much as possible for the rest of the week.

We moved on to other scripts and continued to break stories. It was another few days before I could summon up the courage to say something in the room again.

One day I was Xeroxing table read copies when the other writer's assistant came in. She was holding a printout of the remaining script assignments. She handed it to me and I scanned it eagerly.

My name was listed next to episode twenty.

"I'm pissed. I really wanted an assignment," she said before walking away. I think I nodded. I don't really remember.

After everyone finished lunch, I sought out my boss to thank her.

"Don't let me down," she said.

That night, I called my mom to tell her the good news. It was hard explaining to her what it meant. Finally, I made her understand when I mentioned the extra dough I'd be paid to write the script. That made her happy. Over the course of the weekend, I called everyone I knew, even an old girlfriend who could have cared less. When I hung up, I giggled to myself. I was on top of the world.

The next week my boss called me into her office.

"I have to re-assign your script," she said.

I was too stunned to respond.

"The studio is pressuring me to use someone from outside. Guild regulations."

It was true. The Writer's Guild of America had union rules about it but hardly ever enforced it. Every show I knew hired their assistants. For some reason, this year, the guild was keeping a closer eye on the whole thing.

"I'm sorry," the SR said. "We won't forget about you next year though."

I slinked out of the room, devastated. I tried to imagine how I was going to tell my mom the news given the fact that she'd probably already told all of her friends.

I went to the cramped writer's assistants' office and told my compadre down there.

"Aw, that sucks," she said. Her insincerity was overwhelming.

I felt like dead man walking for the next week. The following Wednesday, the freelancer who was writing my episode showed up. The first time he asked me to get him a Snapple, I felt like someone had stabbed me in the heart.

In the end, his freelance episode was nearly entirely rewritten in the room. I cringed through every aggravating moment of it.

We finished the season and I started bugging my agent again to see if he could get me something for the upcoming staffing season. I promised him a new spec, lying about having one nearly finished when I hadn't even started it.

The wrap party was at some bowling alley in the Valley. I went with the sole purpose of pinning down my boss on her vague promise.

She'd had at least a couple of drinks by the time I'd caught up with her in private.

"Don't worry," she said. "I don't think we're coming back next season."

My jaw dropped.

"I found out on the way over here." She told me the network had pretty much decided already to pull the plug.

I went back to the party and looked around. Sure enough the mood in the room was somber. My boss wanted to make sure we were all together when we found out instead of just getting a phone call weeks down the line. This way we could all have as much time as possible to find a new gig.

Spring ended, and once again, my prospects were somewhere between slim and none. I'd hurried through a spec and it showed. I'd gotten no interviews for staff anywhere. Once again, I was looking for a writer's assistant gig. I made calls to everyone I knew and people I didn't know.

I called everyone who was on staff of my previous show to see where they were ending up. Every one of them was nice to me. One guy, a co-producer who had been a buddy to me, spilled a secret.

He told me the studio hadn't pressured my boss to take me off the assignment. He said she'd put me on the assignment briefly, knowing she'd give it to someone else a week later. I asked him how he knew that. He said she'd confided in one of the co-EP's who later told him. He said she dangled the carrot in front of me only to jerk it away, because she didn't like me.

In the end, he said he was telling me all this for my own good, so I wouldn't waste my time calling her up looking for a job. The underlying message was he was also telling me, in not so many words, to keep my mouth shut next time. I thanked him a dozen times. He ended the call by telling me he'd keep his ear to the ground if something came up.

As the next couple of weeks passed, I was forced to get a job doing food delivery to keep afloat. My mother began calling every other day to convince me I could start a new life back home. The thought made me shudder. I had made my bed, I was going to sleep in it until they dragged me out kicking and screaming.

I chased every two-bit lead for a gig. I looked online, I looked in Backstage, desperately trying to find a way back into the business.

One night, I couldn't take it anymore. I dug up my old phone sheet and looked up the SR's name. Underneath, was the listing for her assistant. I checked my watch and dialed the number.

The assistant was home. He and I hadn't really talked much during my tenure on the show other than when I'd drop off scripts to his desk or when he'd drop by the Xerox room to bum smokes from my surly compadre.

I came right out and asked him if he'd heard what my buddy the co-producer had told me.

"I didn't hear anything," he said.

I had no choice other than to believe him. He then told me he was also out of work. His boss, my old boss, had checked herself into a fairly well-known rehab center for addiction to alcohol and Vicodin. She was to finish up a five-week program and would be returning home soon. Her assistant told me she'd been a pretty big mess for the last six months. I could tell in his voice he'd regretted letting that slip after it came out of his mouth.

He asked what I was doing and I lied, not wanting to tell him about my joe job. He said he had an interview with an agency to be an assistant there. We wished each other luck.

As the summer came, I couldn't even get my agent to return my calls anymore. I was resigned to the fact I'd be delivering food for the time being. I couldn't even get motivated to try my hand at a new spec.

One night, after work, I stopped at my favorite newsstand on La Cienega and bought a copy of *Rolling Stone* and *Guns & Ammo*. I went home to my tiny apartment and found what I was looking for.

The next day I dug out my call sheet from the show and copied my old boss' address onto the front of an envelope. I put no return address. I put a stamp on the front and dropped it in a mailbox on my route during work. I could only hope my old boss would open it to find the two ads I'd torn out for Jack Daniels and Remington shotguns and the typewritten note that said: "Choose one or the other and do us all a favor."

THE EXTREMELY FAMOUS ACTRESS (EFA)

I was the fifth assistant my boss the EFA ever had. The very first one she hired must have been some kind of saint/miracle worker because everything I ever did was held up to comparison. To make things worse, my boss was still close to the first assistant, now a successful talent manager, who called on occasion and spoke very condescendingly to me about how things should be done.

Because of my dreams of moving up to greater heights in "the biz," I put up with it. It's called, "paying your dues."

Last year, I was woken up at four a.m. by a phone call letting me know my grandfather had suddenly passed away. I say suddenly, because although he was seventy, he'd been in great health. He ate right, played tennis three times a week on two reconstructed knees, and was known to go dancing on Saturday nights. I was devastated. My grandfather practically raised me. He was the one who encouraged me to go to Hollywood after college to live my dreams when everyone else back home told me I'd be better off staying in Michigan and finding a husband. As soon as I got off the phone with my aunt, I sat bawling my eyes out until I could gather myself enough to call and book a plane ticket home.

I was at LAX by six and had checked my bags when it dawned on me that I had to let my boss know what had happened. I knew I couldn't call her at home at this hour so, as best as I could, with tears streaming down my cheeks, I left a message on the office voicemail.

Because of the stopover in Phoenix, my plane didn't land until close to two p.m. L.A. time. When I couldn't find my aunt at the airport, I turned my phone on to call her. My message indicator told me I had voicemail. Thinking it was my family, I checked it. It was my boss.

"Where the hell are you?" she was asking me. "I'm in the car on my way to a meeting in Santa Monica and I can't remember the address."

Suddenly, I realized she probably never went into the office. She never got my message. I was about to call her when my aunt showed up. As soon as I saw her, she threw her arms around me and we both cried like babies right there in the airport.

Once we got in the car, my aunt began talking about everything. About how she'd just seen my grandfather yesterday and he looked fit as a fiddle. About how he just died in his sleep, peacefully. Suddenly, I remembered I was going to call my boss. I dialed her cell phone and because of spotty reception, I was cut off twice before I could get the chance to tell her what had happened.

"Sweetie, that's terrible," my boss said.

"I'm in Michigan," I told her. There was silence on the other end. I thought we'd been cut off again.

"Hello?" I asked.

"I'm here." I could tell my boss was annoyed. "You should have told me you were going to be out of the office."

I explained to her that I'd left a message on the office voicemail.

"But I never check that," she said. "That's what I have you for." After a long sigh: "I wonder what other messages are on there that I missed today?"

I could see my aunt was giving me looks from behind the wheel. I wasn't sure if she could hear my boss' voice coming from the earpiece.

"I'll check them and let you know," I told my boss.

I dialed the office voicemail and after my message there were three others. One was from my boss' agent. He was trying to set up a lunch for him and her to get together. My boss didn't take too kindly to the fact she'd missed this call. I told her I was pretty sure he meant lunch a couple of weeks from now. She made me call him back in L.A. He was out so I gave the assistant my cell phone number. When I called my boss back to say I'd left word, she asked when I'd be returning to my job. I told her I wasn't sure. I'd just gotten here and didn't even know when the funeral was. When I said that out loud, I burst into tears. My boss told me not to worry.

When I got to my aunt's house, the rest of my family was already there. I'd no sooner dumped my bags, when they started barraging me with questions about my boss. An older cousin of mine, who had always been a big tabloid reader, began hounding me about every single rumor she'd read to the point that I had to keep ducking her. One of my best friends from high school, who now taught special education kids in our hometown, found out I was home and came over. We sat in my aunt's backyard, smoking cigarettes and crying our eyes out. I asked a thousand questions about her job since I didn't feel like thinking about anything having to do with my life. Sometime around the third cigarette, she asked:

"So, what's she really like?"

I thought about it for a second. "Horrible," I told her.

"You really should move home," she said. Even though I couldn't stand my boss, the thought of moving back here made me shiver.

My aunt was serving up a dinner she cooked for everybody when my boss' agent called. The reception was awful. He said to tell my boss he wanted to do lunch a week from today. I told him I was out of town, but I'd relay the message. He hung up without saying goodbye. I called my boss and thankfully got her cell phone's voicemail. I told her about lunch. After that I decided to turn off my phone.

The next morning, I had to go to the funeral home with my aunt to deliver a suit for my grandfather. On the way, I made the mistake of turning on my phone. I had two messages. The first one was from my boss. She was frantic about something.

I called her at home. She was in tears. Her indoor cat had gotten out somehow and was now missing. Along with the housekeeper, she had mounted a search around her neighborhood to no avail.

"She's only a baby. She can't protect herself out there."

Being that the cat had scratched the hell out of my arms on more than one occasion, I was hoping my boss was wrong. "I wish you were here to help," my boss said. "When are you coming back?"

I told her my grandfather's funeral was tomorrow, and that I had a flight booked for Sunday, two days after that.

Silence on the other end.

"Don't worry," my boss said. "Everything will be okay."

When I hung up, I wasn't sure if she was directing that comment to me or to her, though I had a feeling it was the latter.

The day of my grandfather's funeral, I was a wreck. During the service, I cried so hard my eyes hurt. Here was the man who encouraged every dream I'd ever had, and I never got a chance to say goodbye to him, or tell him one last time how much I loved him. I was so wrecked I don't even remember the graveside service at all.

Everyone went back to my aunt's house afterwards and, because I'd asked her to tell everyone not to bombard me with questions about my famous boss, most people gave me my space. An uncle of mine began telling funny stories about my grandfather, keeping everyone in stitches. Nearly everyone there told me that he'd never die if I kept him in my heart.

Shortly after people began leaving late that afternoon, I answered my aunt's ringing phone to find my boss on the other end. She'd called directory assistance to track me down.

"Your cell phone was off," she said.

I told her my grandfather's funeral had been that morning.

"Well, at least that's behind you," she said. She broke down and told me a neighbor had found what was left of her cat. The poor thing had apparently been attacked by a coyote. My boss began bawling.

"I can't handle death," she said. "I don't know how you do it."

She said there was going to be a memorial service at her house on Sunday and asked if I could be there. I told her my plane was coming into LAX late that night.

Silence on the other end.

"Can you change your flight?" she begged. "I'm going to have a lot of people here." Her "memorial" was going to be at one, which meant I'd either have to take the red-eye or fly out the next day. Usually, I'm quick on my feet, but I wasn't in mental shape to talk my way out of it this time.

"It'd cost me a lot to change my flight," I told my boss.

"That's okay," she said. "I'll pay for it."

I realized I'd screwed up. I scrambled for an excuse and told her I'd have to check with my aunt because I wasn't sure if I was needed to go over my grandfather's estate.

"He couldn't have had that much," my boss said. She was right, but I was getting annoyed and I wanted to get off the phone. I told her I'd call her back.

I stormed into the kitchen where I found my aunt going over some of my grandfather's personal papers. I told her I didn't think I could go back to my job. My boss was probably one of the most awful people I'd ever met.

"People like that are very lost," my aunt said. "That's why they crave so much validation." In the case of my boss, I couldn't have summed it up better in one sentence if I'd taken a year to think about it. I told my aunt about what my boss wanted me to do. I said I wasn't going to do it.

"Maybe she really needs you there," my Aunt said.

No more than five minutes had passed since I'd spoken with my boss when the phone rang again. I picked it up to find my boss' former first assistant on the line.

"I'm helping out while you're gone," she explained in a passive-aggressive way that was supposed to make me feel guilty. "I booked your plane flight."

I told her I was still talking to my aunt about whether or not I should stay until Sunday.

"I'll wait," the first assistant said.

I covered the phone with my hand. My aunt, who'd heard my end of the conversation and understood what was going on, nodded to me and waved her hand as if to say, "it's okay, go." I told the former first assistant that I'd be on the Saturday flight.

In the morning, my aunt took me to the airport. She hugged me and told me it meant everything to her that I'd been home. I cried and promised to see her again at Thanksgiving. When I hugged her goodbye, I couldn't let her go for several minutes.

I slept nearly the entire flight back to L.A., got my car from long-term parking and made it to my apartment feeling exhausted. I dropped my suitcase on my bed and noticed I had several messages on my answering machine. Two were from my boss, looking for me on the day I left. One, which made me cry, was from a close friend who'd heard the news and was sending her condolences. One was from my aunt telling me again that she loved me and missed me already. The last message was from my boss' former first assistant.

"(EFA's name deleted) wants you to get to her house by noon to help set up. And also could you pick up six bags of ice, paper towels and cups?"

THE DIRECTOR ON THE VERGE (DOV)

Truly it was a big deal. My boss was a DOV. His first major motion picture was about to open. Things around our Spartan office were out of control in the days leading up to the big date. We were getting flooded by concerned calls from execs who were fretting over a fairly negative review that had popped up on a major online site. My boss had been editing the film to the last possible second. Tapes were flying in and out, the phones were blowing up every five minutes.

And in the midst of this, my boss wanted his parents to fly in for opening day. Not the premiere, because as my boss told me the lights and the excitement would probably kill them. He was most likely right. His parents were both almost eighty.

Because I had spoken to his mother on the phone several times (at least twenty calls that week to make sure every detail of the trip was accounted for), I drew the plum assignment of meeting them at the airport.

Friday arrived and the office was buzzing by eight a.m. The first showings of my boss' movie were about to seat on the East Coast and we waited with abated breath as to how the crowds were looking in New York, Boston and Philadelphia. By eight-thirty, my boss was into his third Venti half-caf, pacing the carpet, pacing the parking lot and chomping his Nicorette gum like his jaw was in overdrive. The first few reports weren't stellar. The number of people who ditched school or work, or even the unemployed weren't turning up in droves for the early screenings. I could see the look in my boss' eyes that said he was contemplating calling his agency to book him another shoe commercial before word leaked out that his movie was a bomb.

Of course, I got out late from the office and had to drive ninety miles-an-hour to LAX to get his parents. The whole time hoping like hell their flight would be late.

I screeched into a parking space at short-term and dashed through the American terminal like O.J. Simpson on meth. (This was back in the day when you could meet your party at the gate.) I arrived panting and huffing, my lungs burning to see what appeared to be the last few passengers deplane, and to my chagrin, my boss' parents were nowhere in sight.

I began to panic. I tried to find someone who could tell me if they were on the plane, but everyone who saw me with my hair flying all directions, my shirt soaked through with sweat, avoided me like the plague. I was told more than once to go check in baggage claim, but I remembered telling my boss' father (several times) that I would meet them at the gate. My mind raced through anxious thoughts of having to call my boss and telling him, especially in his state of stress, that I had lost his parents. It made my sphincter tight.

At the point at which I was about to have them paged, out from the jet way came two elderly people; the last two passengers on board. To my immediate relief, I had found them.

My boss's mother greeted me with a hug, though I could tell she was loathe to touch my sweaty shirt. My boss' father said only three words to me: "I gotta pee."

Degenerative arthritis had taken a toll on the old man's knees, and he moved with a speed one could only describe as "glacial." Though I didn't time it, my best estimate is that it took us ten minutes to get to the nearest men's room.

After what seemed like twenty minutes of small talk with my boss' mother (the weather, the trip, their cab ride to the airport, the weather again, her vegetable garden, the movie's opening weekend gross estimates), the old man came out of the bathroom with a look of relief on his face. He switched his cane to his left hand and extended his right. I shook it, feeling the dampness that I hoped was only water and soap residue.

I collected their bags (luckily they had packed light) and got them into my car. (Unfortunately, I had a two-door and didn't even think of how much that would be a problem while carrying octogenarians.) We hit a fair amount of traffic going back to the office and all my boss' mother could comment on was how she could never live here. She asked me where I was from (common assumption that everyone in L.A. is a transplant). When I told her I was a SoCal native, she looked at me with sadness.

"So you don't know any better," she told me. I refrained from telling her that was the story of my life.

Back at the office, my boss was in full-lather. Early afternoon estimates were on target. There was lots of press on the release and several TV reviewers had given it high marks. My boss' mother was thrilled. His father turned to me and asked where the toilet was.

By evening, a celebratory mood had broken out in the office. On the East Coast there were people lined up for the seven p.m. screenings, and the nine o'clock and later shows were looking good to be sold out. My boss was into his second bottle of wine before the sun had set.

As I prepared myself to escort my boss' folks to the early evening show at the closest megaplex, my boss took me aside and handed me a hundred bucks to take a cab instead of my car. Apparently his mother said something about a "funny smell" in my Civic.

We arrived at the theatre with plenty of time to spare. My boss was somewhere across town with his model/actress girlfriend-of-the-week, popping into showings of his movie, and had threatened to show up (though I knew that meant he wouldn't). I was on my own and praying for smooth sailing.

We stopped at the box office, and I got a pair of those headphones for the hard-of-hearing for my boss' parents to use. We all made pit stops at our respective restrooms. I watched as my boss' father washed his hands afterwards without soap.

Though there was a line to get into the movie, we managed to kill time by talking about the weather, the cab ride to the theatre, how thin my boss looked and the estimated Friday night box office grosses. My boss's mother made it a point to talk loud enough so those around her knew her son had directed the movie they were about to see (either that or think she was a complete loony). My boss' father just nodded his head and grumbled about getting a good seat.

I watched as the previous show's crowd exited the theatre. Most seemed pleased. I only overheard one person tell their companion they didn't like it. A lot of people talked about the twist at the end and I could actually see those in our line either craning to hear or turn away from hearing. I could tell the movie was going to have a great weekend.

Finally, we were allowed into the theatre. My boss' parents wanted to sit in the very back, on the aisle, but those seats filled up before we could get them. We managed to grab the aisle on the third row from the back, which I thought was going to be good enough.

"I hate having people talk behind me," my boss' mother said. I wondered if she would even hear them with the headphones on. I said nothing and nodded in commiseration. I could see my boss' father getting annoyed.

"These are fine," he grumbled with authority, though I got the feeling he was a man who picked and chose his battles accordingly.

To my relief, we sat through twenty minutes of banner ads and trivia questions projected onto the screen in complete silence. My boss' mother had talked nearly non-stop since arriving and had gabbed herself out. I looked over at my boss' dad and could tell I wasn't the only one enjoying the respite.

Finally, the previews started and, after some fumbling, my boss' parents were able to get their headphones on. However when they tried speaking to each other, they had no idea how loud they were talking.

"My headphones are too loud," screamed my boss' father over the din of the Angelina Jolie trailer blasting in his ears. After some more fumbling on my part, I was able to get them to a volume more to their liking. He turned and gave me a big thumbs-up.

The movie started and I could hear the audio blasting from both the theatre's sound system and my boss' mother's headset. I had screened the movie before a number of times, but I was looking forward to seeing it on the big screen and knew the tinny rasp of every noise coming from next to me would be a big distraction. I sighed and resigned myself to my evening.

About twenty minutes into the movie, my boss' father turned to his wife and yelled at about a hundred decibels:

"I gotta pee!"

I squeezed the bridge of my nose. I could tell he had no idea how loud he was talking when he repeated himself.

My boss' wife stood up and helped him out of the darkened theatre. Even his shuffling was loud enough to draw the attention of everyone around us.

Five minutes later, my boss' father returned and I watched as his wife got up again and helped him to his seat, much to the chagrin of those sitting behind us craning to see past his slow moving silhouette.

No more than forty minutes later, just as I was starting to get back into the movie, my boss' dad turns to his wife and shouted.

"I gotta pee again!"

Once more, she helped him up and out of the theatre and I could tell the people sitting behind me were getting irritated.

"Sorry," I whispered to them.

The woman sitting behind me looked at me with disdain, popped her gum and whispered back.

"Hey, could you tell your grandpa to get a fucking diaper and quiet down?"

☆ ☆ ☆ ☆ ☆

THE LIT AGENT (LA)

One of the perks of being the assistant to an LA was the ability to use my job to meet other guys. In a city full of struggling gay writers, most of them as desperate for a break as they were for a piece of ass, this made for plenty of easy pickings.

There were a number of bars down in WeHo that were ground zero for young entertainment-industry types, and on any given Friday or Saturday night, that's where I'd start my hunting. I'd put on a nice shirt and slacks and go in search for that evening's fun. Usually it didn't take too long before I had a hot, willing fish on the hook.

If you look a certain way, meaning if you look like you know how to dress, guys will come and talk to you. In L.A. it hardly ever takes more than sixty seconds of conversation to ascertain what it is that someone aspires to. If I found out they were a wannabe director: pass. Been there, done that. I mean, I like being told what to do in bed, but only to a point. If I found out they were an actor: pass. Well, depending on if it's last call or not. But more often than not, I could spot the writer from across the room. Writers, for some reason, favor shirts that don't tuck in. Some kind of casual chic thing. Writers favor comfortable shoes. Writers, usually ones out on their own, can be often found not talking to anyone else.

"Just taking it all in," would be one of the opening lines I'd use if I found my fish. One of the other ones I'd use would be:

"Read any good books lately?" Once when I was particularly hammered, I flubbed this line and it came out as, "Read any big cocks lately?"

My instincts, especially from working with writers day in and day out, were usually more right than wrong. If he was cute, willing to chat, drinking and trying to find an agent, it was going to be quick work to set the bait. I'd listen to them talk about themselves and wait for the inevitable. The question.

"So what do you do?" they'd eventually ask. When I'd tell them, I'd often see what I came to call "the look." Their eyes would widen, but only slightly as they tried to keep their poker faces. I'd go on and talk about my job and when I'd get to the part about the two big specs my boss sold in the last year, I could almost feel them inching closer to me. If I had a little fishy I really wanted to reel in, I had a move I called "the closer." I'd reach over and lightly touch their arm and say I loved my job because my boss had a reputation of being a "star maker."

And when the time was right, a couple of drinks later I'd tell them, as if it just came to me in a flash of inspiration,

"Hey, maybe I could get my boss to read your stuff."

Game. Set. Match.

And after a few more drinks, back to his place we'd go for a mutually enjoyable time between the sheets. Sometimes, if I really had a good time, I'd even continue the ploy. I'd keep them on the hook for a week or two with promises I never intended to honor. If a cute guy was willing to let me come over and blow him on a regular basis, I'd promise him the world, or at least a shot at getting repped.

But then one day at the office, one of my fish began to call. He was handsome with his dirty blond hair and muscles in all the right places, and perhaps he had sensed I had begun to become bored with him.

Because I was open with where I worked, I was easy to track down. He wanted to know when I'd finally come through on my hollow promises. His spec was ready and he

76

wanted my boss to read it like I had promised all of those times before I'd stuffed his cock into my mouth.

I told him I couldn't talk right now, that I'd call him later after I spoke to my boss about it. I was hoping he'd get the message.

He didn't.

A few days later, he called again. He caught me off guard and I told him to send the script. I added that I would personally put it in front of my boss.

When the script arrived via FedEx, I took one look at it and tossed it in the trash. I wrote a polite letter from my boss passing on his work. I would of course make it look good by waiting two weeks before sending it, though.

But the next week, first thing Monday morning, he called again wanting to know if my boss read it. I told him my boss hadn't come in yet. The fish gave me his home and cell number and told me to call as soon as I knew something. I'd pitched his number a couple of weeks earlier and wasn't really thrilled to have it again. I put on my best sweet voice and promised I'd see to it.

Two days later, when I hadn't called, he called back. I ducked his calls. I realized I had to get rid of him for good. I found the "pass" letter I'd written to him and mailed it out on Friday.

Monday came and there was thankfully no call, but on Tuesday he phoned, very irate.

"You lied to me," he said. I pretended to be surprised at his allegations. He told me he got the letter and that I had promised to get my boss to represent him. I told him I'd only promised to get my boss to read it, but was unsure how much I'd actually crossed that line while drunk. He told me he knew I was bullshitting him because the letter was dated a week *after* he had gotten it. I slapped my forehead. In my haste, I'd forgotten to change it when I'd mailed the kiss-off letter early. I told him that was just a typo. He could smell a rat though.

"You used me," he fumed before hanging up on me.

In a way I was relieved. He'd nearly been stalking me and I figured it was over.

But then over the course of the next week or so, the guy began writing about what I'd done to him on entertainment industry message boards on the Internet. He named me, named my boss and meticulously detailed everything that had happened. When a friend of mine forwarded me one of the postings, I was mortified. Not only because he'd outed me to my peers, but he'd also revealed my perfect little scam. Desperately, I searched for his phone number, then realized I'd tossed it after our last phone call. I tried directory assistance, but got nowhere.

To my horror, not only did the postings get read, but other people added replies; some of them claiming to know me. From the usernames, I couldn't tell if they were writing the truth or not. It didn't matter though. My name had been splashed all over the board and I'd become a big joke. I thought of suing for libel, but everything he'd written about me was true. In a court of law, he'd probably be able to find several other fish to corroborate his story just by asking around the bar where we'd met. My only solace was that my parents, who didn't own a computer, would probably never see this.

But my boss could.

My heart sank. I knew it was probably just a matter of time before someone showed the posting to my boss. I feared the original recap of my indiscretions was already making the rounds in e-mails being forwarded around town. I knew I had only one choice.

I had to tell my boss before he found out from someone else.

The next day I felt sick to my stomach. I waited as long as I could. It was right after lunch and I could sense he was in a decent mood. It was as good as it was going to get.

I went into his office. I closed the door behind me. I mumbled that there was something I had to tell him. He wrinkled his brow. He didn't like surprises.

I told him my softened confession of what I'd done; that I never intended for it to get out of hand, or for his name to come into it in any way. I blabbered on for ten minutes, wringing my hands together the whole time. When I was done I waited for my boss' wrath. He chewed me out for five minutes for getting his name dragged into it by virtue of my association.

After lunch, he called me into his office. I had a feeling this was it, he was going to fire me. I was prepared to take my sacking like a man.

"You really met writers this way and fucked them?" he asked.

Sheepishly, I nodded, waiting for him to lower the boom.

Instead he chuckled.

"You fucking perv," he grinned. "You are going to make a great agent someday."

THE TELEVISION STUDIO EXECUTIVE (TSEX)

Two months into my job working the desk for a TSEX, I thought I had the routine down. Nothing phased me. Problem was, I was so busy patting myself on the back for a job well done, and dreaming of the day when I could get promoted, that I never saw the eight-ton elephant in the middle of the room. My boss' behavior had become more erratic, and as a good assistant, I covered for him without even thinking about why. One time, he didn't show up for work, and I had to call the big boss' assistant to say my boss had come down with a stomach bug. Another time, when he missed an important meeting, I told someone my boss' kid had to be taken to the hospital with a broken arm.

Stupid me, I was so proud of being able to make up lies on my feet like that, that I had to tell him what I had done. He looked at me, kind of stunned as I documented the half-dozen or so whoppers I had told other people to explain his absences. I thought he was going to explode. Finally, he let out a long rolling laugh. He actually slapped me on the back and, with a wink, told me I had done a good job.

Two weeks later, he handed me a videotape case and told me to overnight it to someone I had never heard of before. He said it was really important and that I was to drop everything I was doing, pack it up right away, and personally walk it down to the drop box.

I looked at the clock. It was three. The last pickup was five-thirty. He got cross with me and said to just do what he said and take it down now and then stormed back into his office. I shrugged. As I slid the tape case into a padded envelope, I stopped. I had sent dozens of videotapes, handled hundreds of tape cases, and they all had one thing in common: they rattled.

This one didn't. The weight didn't even feel right. Before even thinking of what I was about to do, I opened the case to look. You can imagine my surprise when I found the two sandwich baggies of white powder inside.

THE BIG FILM DIRECTOR (BFD)

I'm sure it's not uncommon to be in an industry where the boss is trying to get into your pants, but the time he bought me a car should have been my first clue. I could tell my mother was a bit suspicious, but my hundred thousand miler Ford Escort just bit the dust and I didn't have the money to replace it. After all, he was a BFD. I'd seen his seven-figure tax returns. I just figured he was being a nice guy.

It was a twelve thousand dollar gift. I told my mother that he'd bragged of dropping twice that much one night in Vegas before even finishing his first comped whiskey on the rocks. Besides, he was very married and doted over his kids. When he wrote me that check, there was never any indication of obligation. No wink, no sly grin. Just a fatherly admonition to make sure I buy something that'll get me to work. I was so grateful I cried right there in his office.

About three months later, the phone calls started.

I'd become used to him calling me at home. I was his assistant, I knew where he last left his Palm Pilot. I knew when the new meeting times were. That was part of the job. Having my phone ring at two a.m. and hearing him sounding sloshed on the other end, wasn't.

"I can't find my car," he told me. I could hear the traffic in the background.

I squeezed my eyes shut. Ugh. "Where are you?"

I had to go get him. His Benz had been towed. I asked him why he didn't call his wife. He told me she would have his ass if she found out about the car. He made me swear not to tell anybody.

It was the first of our many "secrets."

Soon, he was confiding a lot more to me. One day he made me close the door to his office. "Sit down," he said.

I thought I was about to be fired. Instead, he gazed up and I could see his tired eyes.

"My wife and I are separating," he said.

I gasped. I couldn't believe it. He said they had been having trouble for a while. All I could think of was the time I was ten and my mother told me she and my dad were getting a divorce.

"I'm really sorry," I said. I meant it, too.

That night he called me from the car on the way home.

And then again right around ten o'clock.

In the office, things were totally normal. He yelled at writers. He yelled at the studio. Only I could see the fraying around the edges, but we never talked about it during the day.

But at night it was another story. He was calling me every night now, sometimes two or three times. Often I could hear the clink of ice in a glass in the background and I imagined him sitting in dark in the office in his guesthouse after his kids had gone to bed. We talked about his life; about my life. I learned that as a kid he wanted to be a park ranger. Somehow, I thought that was funny and he laughed when I giggled. It was the first time I thought I could hear him smile over the phone.

The next night he showed up at my door, under the influence of something. He was shaking. I had a sinking feeling in the pit of my stomach, but I couldn't let him stand out there. I let him in. He asked for a glass of water that he never drank. Instead, he paced, running his hand through his hair. I told him to calm down. Finally, he sat down and let it all out.

"My wife and I had a pretty bad argument," he said. He couldn't even look at me. "It was about you."

A red flag the size of China popped up in my head. The hesitant warning of my mother over me taking the twelve grand for the car played back inside my brain.

"She knows we've been talking on the phone every night," he said, using *we* in such a way that made me seem to be more of an accomplice than an enabler. "She wants me to fire you."

The vertigo I was feeling was the rug being pulled out from under me. "That's crazy!" I blurted. "We were just talking."

"Not exactly," he said. The room was spinning. I felt like George Jetson trapped on that out of control treadmill, unable to catch my next step.

That's when he said: "When I called you last night, she caught me..." He hesitated. And I knew what he was about to say by the somewhat non-embarrassed look on his face. "...playing with myself."

Jane, stop this crazy thing.

I had been thrown into a state of repulsion so deep I was paralyzed. That's when I felt his hand drop onto my knee. It felt like a cold, dead squid against my skin.

"I think I love you," he said, looking like more like a heartsick teenage boy than someone ten years my senior.

"I... I just don't feel that way about you," I pulled my knee away. His limp hand fell off it.

"Please, I'm so confused." He began weeping on my couch. I wasn't sure whether to go get a box of tissues or my pepper spray. For the next hour, I listened to him ramble on about what he perceived as the desperate state of his life, his lack of a soul and his growing love for me since the day I was hired. Coming, of course, in between gales of uncontrollable sobbing. I pretended as well as I could to listen, but my synapses had been blown to smithereens already. In my head I made my grocery list and nodded whenever there was a lull in his monologue. I was hoping my phone would ring, that my building would catch on fire, anything to use an excuse to get him out of here.

No such luck though.

After a fourth trip to my bathroom, he mumbled some last few incoherent, and somewhat angry-sounding, words, tried to kiss me to no avail, then left. I was going to offer to call him a cab, but was afraid showing concern would be misinterpreted as a sign of affection. I double locked my door and watched through the peephole to make sure he wasn't going to come back.

THE SENIOR STUDIO EXECUTIVE (SSEX)

Thanks to a friend who had moved out to California a year before me, I got a job as the second assistant to a SSEX. My qualifications, he said, made me the ideal person for the job. I never realized my Ivy League degree in English would be my ticket into the entertainment industry.

I showed up for work, ready to learn the ropes, ready to make copies, run for coffee, pick up dry cleaning, whatever it took to work my way up the ladder from my entry level position. My boss was out half of the day in meetings, and I waited for the first assistant to teach me how to answer the phones correctly since I figured that would be my domain as well.

"That's *my* job," she said. "(SSEX's name deleted) will explain your job when he gets back."

After lunch, my boss finally arrived, storming into the office, shaking my hand for the briefest of moments before disappearing behind closed doors. It was the first time I had even met him, since my job interview had been done over the phone. While he was briefed on the goings-on by the first assistant, I sat out front, flipping through the same copy of Variety I had practically worn out while waiting all morning to be told what was expected of me.

Finally, the first assistant came out.

"He's ready for you now."

Entering my boss' office, I was immediately floored by how big it was. Photos, awards, movie posters adorned nearly every inch of wall space. My boss gestured to the seat in front of his massive desk.

"Sorry, it's been a crazy day," he explained. "Some heads may roll because of the (movie title deleted) debacle."

Immediately, I thought of my job security. Was I going to be out of a gig before it even started? My boss, however, could read my mind.

"Don't worry," he said. "Not my head."

I smiled, not wanting to tell him it wasn't *his* head I had been worried about. I could tell by the grin on his face he was happy about whomever it was that was going to be fired.

"Your qualifications are outstanding," he told me. "I'm very pleased you took this job."

All of a sudden, I had visions I was being groomed for some kind of executive position, that maybe nobody asked me to fetch lunch or deliver tapes because that would be beneath me. I was to be vaulted above the average assistant. No wonder the first assistant had been so cold to me all morning long.

My boss took a family photo from the credenza behind his desk. He handed it to me. Along with himself and a beautiful wife I thought I might have recognized from an old TV show, were two children; a boy and a girl. Everyone was smiling.

"These are my kids," my boss explained. "They haven't been doing so well in school, and that's exactly where you come in..."

I could feel the key to the executive washroom slipping from my fingers. He explained I was to be a tutor to his son and daughter.

"Well, not exactly a tutor..." my boss went on. I had heard of such things before, but never thought in a million years I'd be asked to do what he wanted.

"Help me out and I can really help your career," he said. "You want to be a screenwriter, right?"

He had me hook, line and sinker. He rolled names of mega-agents and producers who all begged to do business with him. I thought of the doors he could open for me with one phone call and any resistance I had just melted away.

"I'm your man," I told him. I could see his grin widen even further.

The next day I showed up at his Malibu Colony home sometime after three in the afternoon. The housekeeper let me in. I had been expected. She showed me up the steps to a closed bedroom door. From behind, I could hear the booming sounds of the new Slipknot CD coming from a stereo inside. The housekeeper motioned for me to knock. I did. There was no answer. I waited and knocked again, this time louder.

The door opened and the annoyed face staring back at me from inside looked little like the one in the family portrait my boss showed me. My guess was the photo had been taken at least two years previous. The kid I was staring at looked like a total stoner. He stared at me blankly for a moment as I introduced myself. Finally, it hit him.

"Right, you're the dude my dad hired." He opened the door and let me in. The smell of pot in his room was so strong, I thought I was already getting a contact high from just being in there. The room was a sty. Clothes everywhere. A collection of guitars, some in cases, some not, littering the floor. I had a feeling the housekeeper hadn't been in there for years. My boss' son flopped down on the bed and told me I could sit at his desk. I achieved my proudest moment of the day when I managed to push aside the dirty t-shirts and underwear on the chair without showing too much revulsion.

My boss' son picked up a guitar and began to lazily pick at it. Though I was no musician, I could tell the instrument was badly out of tune.

"A Separate Peace," he said. "I have a five page paper on it due Friday."

Vaguely, I remembered it from my own ninth-grade English class nearly a decade earlier. I asked what I should have figured would be a stupid question.

"Did you read it?"

His response sounded like a steam vent momentarily releasing pressure. *Pfffft.* "I don't like to read," he said. "Gives me a headache."

I bit my lip. "What about music?"

"Don't need to read music. Rock and roll's not about reading music," he said, not looking at me and picking the guitar. Obviously to him, rock and roll wasn't about tuning either.

"Bring it by on Thursday night," he told me. It was an order as good as one being handed down by his father. He picked at his guitar and ignored my presence. I could tell he was done with me for the time being.

"Sure," I told him and left the room.

On my way home I stopped and picked up a copy of *A Separate Peace,* and then spent the rest of the evening boning up on it. I had just about two days to write a paper. In school, I hated having to do book reports. Now I was back in the ninth grade, ghostwriting for my boss' stoner dipshit son. I swallowed my pride. There were worse ways to make a buck.

The paper I delivered Thursday afternoon as promised was brilliant. I focused on the book's themes of denial and irresponsibility; hoping somehow the general message would be subconsciously absorbed by my boss' son. He took the pages from me and didn't even look at them.

"Cool," he said. I figured that would have to suffice as a thank you.

My boss' daughter stopped me in the hallway.

"Spanish-American War," she said pushing a large history textbook into my hand. "I don't have time to learn this."

I followed her back to her room where she showed me a color wheel she was spending all her waking hours working on. Her father had helped her start her own makeup line. She was the second girl in her class to do so.

"This red makes me look like an autumn, not a summer," she pointed to a shade of lipstick she was hoping to introduce before the end of the semester. I had no idea what she was talking about. The gist of what she wanted boiled down to a five thousand word term paper by the end of next week.

"Besides, who cares about those people anyway? They're all dead," she said.

I took her textbook and left her to the merciless color wheel. The next four days, I spent the mornings at the office making copies and fetching coffee, and the afternoons in the library researching the Battle of Manila Bay and Teddy Roosevelt's famed charge up San Juan Hill. By Monday, I had an outline and by Wednesday, a fairly decent draft. It occurred to me that I hadn't worked on my script for more than a week. I figured there'd be time later.

The term paper, much like my book report, turned out to be a smash success. Both garnered A's (an A- for the book report because I didn't exploit the jealousy angle as much as the teacher wanted). My boss was very pleased. He called me into his office.

"You're a fucking genius," he exclaimed, slapping me on the back. For five minutes, he showered me with praise. I left the office that day on a high. The feeling lasted the entire weekend as I locked myself in my apartment and finished the second act of my screenplay. Things were looking up.

Monday came, and I quietly went about my office duties, awaiting my next ghostwriting assignment. The next day, I was summoned back to my boss' house. His son had a history paper due on the Civil War, which he was pretty sure "happened about fifty years ago." I asked him which part of the war I was supposed to write about.

"Whatever the important part was." He shrugged and mangled the opening riff to "Stairway to Heaven" on his guitar.

"Slavery?"

"What's that?" he asked, not even looking up.

And so my fall and winter went. A book report here, a social studies essay there. My own writing had fallen by the wayside, but I looked at all the time I was clocking at the library as an investment in my future. Besides, I had accumulated a string of A's and B pluses that I was kind of proud of (my paper on Adam Smith's *Wealth of Nations* dwelled a page too long on the issue of public welfare, according to the teacher).

When Christmas vacation arrived, I was relieved to hear neither of my charges had been assigned any reading during their break. While they were off skiing in Vail, I was going to bear down and finally finish my script.

Things were looking up. My boss had given me a hundred dollar Blockbuster gift card, and a fatherly squeeze on the shoulder as he left for his trip.

"You're doing a great job," he said. The first assistant had even started to talk to me like I was a human being. I was happy. My boss' words echoed in my head as I drove home that day.

After an obligatory visit to my folks, I raced back to L.A. to get cracking on my script. I was knee deep into the climax and could smell the end in sight. I fantasized about the connections my boss would be making for me. I kept telling myself Spielberg would be perfect to direct my screenplay.

I typed "Fade Out" the night before my boss was to return. My script was done. I could barely contain my excitement. It had taken the better part of a year to finish my masterpiece. The next morning I went into the office early to make copies.

I prepped a copy for my boss, checking twice to make sure all the pages were in the right order. I was going to wait for the right moment to slip it to him.

He didn't come back the first day, and when he did show up to the office, he was in a terrible mood. The vacation hadn't gone so smoothly. His son had gotten drunk with a few friends ("fuckin' troublemakers," my boss said) and had gotten arrested for being drunk and disorderly in a movie theatre ("Not one of my films, thank Christ," my boss said). The extra day in Vail was so they could attend the arraignment.

I hid my script away. I could see my boss was in no mood. It took me a year to write a draft. I could wait another week.

The second week back from break, my duties as a ghostwriter returned full swing (ten-pager on the themes of hypocrisy of civilized society in *Huck Finn*). I was biding my time but my boss' mood had turned even more foul. The new production executive they had hired back when I started was supposedly campaigning behind closed doors to replace my boss. According to hushed gossip I was hearing from the first assistant, there were plenty of open ears up and down the ladder willing to consider the regime change.

My boss went on the warpath, spending even less time at the office and more time taking meetings across town. When I heard the focus of his strategy was to find the next *can't-miss* project, my throat went dry. I felt I had the answers to his (and my problems) in a manila envelope in my bag.

I made up my mind. I was going to give my script to my boss the next day.

The following afternoon, my boss returned from lunch and ensconced himself in his office to return calls. I asked the first assistant to let me know when he was off the phone (I told her I had to talk to him about something concerning his kids). I waited, butterflies in my stomach, for her signal.

"He's off," she told me. "But he's expecting another call in five minutes."

Five minutes. That's all I'd need. I grabbed my script and went into his office.

Gently, I knocked on the door. My boss looked up at me and waved me in. He asked how the papers were coming along. I told him fine. He began to thank me again for the job I was doing. He said the boost in grades helped his daughter to get more confident about her cosmetics line (I refrained from telling him it probably had to do with the fact that it was because I was freeing her up from having to do her own work). As he talked, I nervously watched the clock on the credenza behind him. One minute passed, then two, then three. My time was running short.

Finally when I had a chance, I told him why I wanted to talk to him.

"I finished my script," I said, proudly.

He blinked, his poker face faltering for the briefest of moments. "Great," he said, taking it from me. "I'll read it this weekend."

The phone rang and the first assistant buzzed him. His call had come in. I thanked him again and left his office. I was pretty sure I was smiling.

Monday came. I had finished the *Huck Finn* paper and felt I had nailed it. My boss was out of the office again, and I nervously awaited what I expected to be my coronation as the next hot young screenwriter. Tuesday came and he swept into the office, spending most of the day on the phone.

"He must be making a deal," the first assistant told me over coffee. My heart leapt into my mouth. Was it my script he was wheeling and dealing? Why wouldn't he tell me? Was he treading lightly so I wouldn't be disappointed if it didn't happen? Still, I wanted to know.

Wednesday passed and so did Thursday. My boss spent little time in the office. I was dying inside. I could barely sleep at night. Every time I saw a BMW or Porsche on the street that weekend, I imagined that next week I'd be waltzing into a dealership somewhere to buy one of my own.

On Monday I got into the office a bit late (traffic) to find the first assistant awaiting my arrival.

"He wants to talk to you," she said. "Right now."

I felt myself actually trembling at her words.

I entered my boss' office and he waved me in as he finished a call. He reached into his attaché case and pulled out a document and dropped it on his desk. At first I thought it was a contract: one of the thick, juicy Hollywood "rich and famous" variety. But then I saw the "F" in red marker on the top right.

It was my *Huck Finn* paper.

"What the fuck is this?" my boss shouted. I picked up the paper. How? It was perfect.

"I don't understand," I said.

"Are you some kind of idiot?"

"I don't understand…"

"You wrote it too good! The teacher knew the moment she read it that (son's name deleted) couldn't have written this!"

The blood rushed from my face. He was right. This was something I would have been proud to hand in at Cornell.

"Luckily, his teacher thinks he bought it from one of those term paper services. (son's name deleted) has one chance to rewrite the paper. You have a week to fix this."

And that's when I noticed it...

My script was still on his desk where he had put it. I could tell because I had gone ahead and written the name along the spine with a Sharpie. It was buried under a stack of at least a half-dozen other scripts. Close to the bottom. I wanted to ask if he had gotten a chance to read it, but knew this wasn't the right time.

With a flick of his hand, my boss dismissed me.

As I got to the door, he said one last thing: "Dumb it down this time."

I finished my office duties in silence, brooding over the fact that I would have to write this paper a second time. I went back to the library and researched a new angle for Huck Finn. The problem was dumbing it down. It went against every instinct I had. I loaded it with every cliché I could find. Every poorly written observation a high-school kid would use, cut me like a knife. I strayed from an A paper as far as I dared. I rewrote it twice to make sure I had dumbed it down enough. The night before it was due, I drove over to my boss' house and gave it to his son.

"You better not have fucked me," my boss' son said as he took the paper from me and shut the front door in my face. I left, certain that he probably wouldn't even read it.

The paper pulled a B-minus. Not too good and not too bad. I was still persona-non-grata at the office though. My boss was still chilly to me. If I had to go into his office to bring him something, he barely spoke two words to me. Every time I went into his office I saw my script still sitting at the bottom of the pile. The worst part was that I knew the ones on top of it were changing. He was reading, just not my script.

Sundance came and my boss jetted off to Park City. I went into his office to retrieve an itinerary, and to my surprise, all the scripts in the pile were gone. I asked the first assistant and she shrugged.

"Probably took them with him," she said.

My hopes raised again. I had another book report to write (*The Great Gatsby*), and a four-pager on the Bill of Rights. I worked hard, but tempered my word choices to eliminate anything remotely collegiate. I stayed at the library until they kicked me out, the whole time trying to keep my eyes on the prize.

My boss returned from Park City and again I waited to hear his verdict on my script. Again, nothing. One week passed, then a second. During the third week, I found a perfect opportunity to bring it up. My efforts on another Social Studies paper paid off. His daughter's grade average had risen to a solid B. Her teachers were praising her "increased effort." He and I both knew I was the reason. His daughter hadn't thought about more than her new mascara line since Christmas.

Just as I was about to ask my boss about my script, he turned to me.

"I gave your script to someone at (large agency name deleted). I think he wants to talk to you."

I couldn't believe it. My ship was coming in. I waited for days, hyperventilating at every ring of the phone, hoping each time it was the agent calling for me. Finally, after two weeks, the agent's assistant buzzed me on my cell phone. I had an appointment to see him that Friday.

As I entered the agent's office I realized he was pretty young. He greeted me and proceeded to talk for five minutes straight about how much he liked my boss. Just at the point I couldn't take it anymore, he changed the subject.

"I liked the writing a lot," he said. My heart skipped a beat. And then with a completely straight face he said: "But the story has a lot of problems."

He took out his copy of the script and handed it back to me.

"As a favor to your boss, I made some notes." He said something after that, but I was so busy trying to keep my poker face that it just went in one ear and out the other. He dismissed me saying he had a meeting to get to. He shook my hand and told me to feel free to send the script back to him after I'd given it a rewrite.

As I got into my car, I cracked open the script. There was red pen everywhere. It looked like an apache massacre.

Honestly, I was crestfallen. It had taken me so long to write it, and I had entered the agent's office thinking I'd be leaving with good news. Instead, I had another rock to roll up the hill. I went home and read through the notes. I wanted to start on the rewrite, but had another paper to ghostwrite for my boss' son. I put my script aside.

As the winter dragged into spring, my efforts to finish my script were sporadic at best. The end of the school term was approaching, and it seemed like my "workload" had doubled. As April came, I felt like my wheels were spinning. My boss' daughter had to write a final term paper about her senior year project: the cosmetics company she started. It was a massive task, practically a thesis paper. I had a month to write it.

I went over to my boss' house and his daughter handed me a shoebox full of scribbled notes, none of which made sense to me. A list of names for a lip gloss on one page, a list of celebrities she would (have her father) approach for endorsements on the other. I knew nothing about cosmetics or what she had been doing. I was completely lost. I tried sitting down with her to get more information, but her cell phone would go off every five minutes. In two hours, we probably spoke for twenty minutes, mostly going over the same things over and over. I retreated to my apartment to mull it over. My education to this point hadn't prepared me for this.

With a week left to go before the paper was due, I panicked. I had four pages at best, about one fifth of the paper done. I had nothing. I went to the library and found a book on makeup icon Max Factor; I went to Macy's and snagged some pamphlets on MAC and Prescriptives. I drank coffee and bullshitted my way through another fifteen (widely-spaced) pages. I delivered the paper the day before it was due. It was received with the same lack of a "thank you" as all of the previous work I'd done.

With summer vacation in sight, I finally could begin thinking about finishing my script again. I began to make notes. I would change the ending again. I had great ideas.

And then the bomb hit.

My boss' new rival had succeeded in undermining my boss' position at the studio. Word was spreading like wildfire that my boss was on the way out. I knew the rumors were true the afternoon I realized the phones weren't ringing as much as usual. A couple of days later, the first assistant confided in me that she had interviewed for another job elsewhere.

"You might want to consider your options before it's too late," she told me. "Looking for a job when you're unemployed is a bad bargaining position."

A week later she was training me to take over for her. She continued to hint I might want to take stock of the fact the ship was indeed sinking. There was even a story in *The Hollywood Reporter* about my boss being on the way out.

The next three weeks were a whirlwind. As the new first assistant, I was now stuck at the office until late. By the time I got home, my head was pounding from rolling calls. I had no motivation to write. On weekends, my boss would hand me a pile of scripts to read. I wondered if he had done this with my script, passing it to the old first assistant for her verdict.

Then one Monday, I came into work. It started as any other day. By lunchtime I had begun packing up the office. Over the weekend, my boss had negotiated his out. The studio would be giving him a production deal and an office on the lot. It was his severance package for being forced out of his job. He came into the office wearing a polo shirt and Dockers instead of his usual suit. He barely spoke to me.

By Thursday I had finished packing everything up. Monday, someone else would be moving in. I had desperately been wondering about my future. I figured my boss would need an assistant at his new shingle. I had to be the first choice for that considering how well I knew the job. I wanted to ask him, but he barely showed his face in the office.

On Friday, as I was getting ready to come in, my phone rang. It was my boss.

"I'm gonna have to let you go," he said. I was too stunned for words. The final term paper I had written about his daughter's cosmetics venture had gotten a D-plus. Suffice to say, he was not pleased. She would still graduate, just barely. I wanted to mention that her B-minus average probably had more to do with my previous efforts, but instead I bit my tongue. He offered to pay me two weeks' severance. I accepted. He wished me luck. At no time, did he ever thank me for what I had done during the school year.

Eventually I found a job as a P.A. It took me two more months to finish my script. I tried calling and e-mailing the agent at (agency name deleted) but never got a response. He had done his favor to me. I was nobody now. I didn't even merit a blow-off e-mail.

A few months later, I was ready to pack it up and move back east, maybe look for a nice teaching job in a small town near a ski resort. As a last ditch effort, I decided I had nothing to lose by contacting my boss to see if I could send him the script. Of course he wasn't in (or wouldn't take my call), so I left my message. To my surprise it turned out the assistant answering the phone was someone I sort of knew from school. He recognized my name. He asked if I could meet for coffee.

The next day he confided in me that my old boss had hired him "based on his education," but he had no idea the job entailed writing all of his brain-dead son's school papers. I told him he was lucky, the daughter had graduated and flown the coop to run her cosmetics company. He told me her venture had run out of gas. She was folding it and had applied to UCLA for the spring semester. When I found out he was the only assistant in the office, I told him he had his work cut out for him.

He stared into his cup of java, obviously rethinking the gig. I asked him what had brought him out to Hollywood. He said he was trying to be a writer.

I wished him good luck.

☆ ☆ ☆ ☆ ☆

THE CONTROVERSIAL MOVIE DIRECTOR (CMD)

I had just broken up with my girlfriend and was planning to spend a Saturday night reading scripts for my boss when my roommate convinced me to go with him to a party being thrown for a girl he knew. When he told me the venue was going to be the house of a pretty famous producer, I decided I couldn't pass it up. We arrived at a "parking area" behind a building not too far from Chateau Marmont. Once there, we had to "check in" with a headset-clad, clipboard-toting security guard who crossed our names off of a list. From there we were allowed into a waiting area where a shuttle van would take us up to the house. Ten minutes later, we were dropped off at the front door of a mansion that must have been worth in the low eight-figures.

We entered, and you could tell immediately this was no ordinary Hollywood weekend kegger. In one room, four bartenders poured free-flowing drinks. In another room, a band, featuring an all-star lineup of guys I recognized from MTV, was setting up to perform. In another was a massive rave with lights and a d.j. spinning trance at a volume I thought was going to split my head open. Everywhere, as far as the eye could see, were actresses. Some I recognized, some who were, as my roommate liked to say, "mattresses" (model/actress/waitress). In the living room, holding court with a bunch of eager listeners was an infamous Hollywood madam who had just recently been released from a brief stint behind bars. By this time, my roommate had disappeared into the rave, most likely to rub up against some of the young talent. I, on the other hand, scored a large scotch rocks from the bar and wandered out back to one of the terraces overlooking a massive garden.

About a minute later, one of the French doors opened behind me and out next to me, also obviously looking for some fresh air, was one of the most famous CMD's in the world. At first, I couldn't believe it, but then after letting him have a peaceful half-minute, I decided I had to say something. I was polite about it. I broke the silence and told him I felt like his last movie, a big-budget sports-themed affair that never quite caught fire at the box-office, was one of the best movies I had seen that year. I told him how the way he shot it really made me feel like I was in the game. His face, placid and tired up to that point, lit up like a Christmas tree.

He thanked me and I could hear the disappointment in his face as he told me how the critics never got it. We then talked about a previous movie of his, an infamous flick that inflamed the media, and he just looked at his shoes and began mumbling how he wasn't even sure if he was any good anymore, or if he was any good to begin with. Here he was, with a stranger he had just met five minutes before, blubbering about quitting the business. I couldn't believe it. I pleaded with him not to, that meeting me proved there were people out there who "got" his work. He thanked me, and when his date, a buxom blonde, came out looking for him holding a pair of drinks, he shook my hand and disappeared back into the party.

I tried looking around for my roommate to tell him what had just happened, but I couldn't find him. Then about an hour later, I saw my buddy, the CMD, coming down the house's back steps by the kitchen. He was having trouble navigating the narrow steps and must have missed one, because he tripped down the last three, barely avoiding a face-plant by landing awkwardly on his feet with a loud bang.

Everyone was watching, and I think he knew it. He grabbed his date and left the house.

THE SOAP STAR (SS)

My boss the SS was a complete germaphobe, and made the mistake of pissing me off once by chewing me out for something I had virtually no control over. I spent a whole night brooding over it before deciding I was going to get him back where it hurt the most.

I waited until he was gone on one of his trips to New York. I had it all planned out. I was going to spread my germs everywhere. I was going to go on a full rampage of filth.

I had debated long and hard that morning as to where my terrorism would begin. As I pulled into his driveway, I decided to start simply. I marched into the bathroom.

He replaced his toothbrush regularly with a brand new Oral B. It was the housekeeper's job to toss the old one away on a weekly basis and replace it with a new one. She had also been instructed to leave the old one in the trashcan so he could double check to make sure it had indeed been replaced. I spied the old Oral B in the can and the new one hanging by the sink, waiting for the master of the house to return. I grinned as I took the new toothbrush from its holder over to the toilet and unzipped my pants, taking great pleasure in pissing all over it before returning it to where it belonged.

It was not uncommon for my girlfriend to come pick me up. That night I told her to swing by early. I greeted her at the front door with a grin and little else. I took her upstairs and we had wild sex on my boss' desk, me taking great pleasure in sitting her bare ass right on his work surface as I pounded into her. When I was done, I had one last thing in mind. I strolled, naked, into the kitchen and opened the fridge. Inside was an already opened bottle of the all-natural and unfiltered juice he consumed religiously. I took the cap off, tilted the contents slightly and thrust my sex-encrusted penis into the mouth of the bottle, recoiling slightly as the cold juice swished around the head of my cock. Satisfied with my deed, I recapped the juice and placed it back in the fridge, label-side out, just as I had found it.

My boss came back home, as expected, and went about his normal routines. In a couple of weeks time, I had come to forgive him for being a prick, and even continued on to work for him for another year. He was still an obsessive freak, but every time I watched him working at his desk, or drink his juice, or if I heard him talking about brushing his teeth, I managed to get through my day a little easier.

THE PRODUCER GETTING DIVORCED (PGD)

The divorce my boss was going through was making her bitchy, to say the least. As the proceedings turned into an all out knock-down, drag-out war, I could see it was inevitable I would be pulled into it somehow.

For the first year I'd worked for her, before she became a PGD, they'd been involved with a film project together based upon an experience he'd had overseas in his younger, crazier days. They fought constantly, bickering not only about married-people things, but also about every little detail concerning the script. At first he'd taken a crack at writing it, secretly pounding away at it until he turned in a bloated two hundred fifty-page draft filled top to bottom with long, droning voice-overs that really went nowhere. After taking another couple of months to try and polish the script, he'd only cut it down to just under two hundred pages. The day she told him they'd have to have someone come in and rewrite it, a total stranger no less, he'd launched a coffee mug at her, or so I was told later.

He'd call the office on a daily basis to yell at her about one thing or another. Even through her closed door I could hear it. She'd scream back at him and during the protracted silences I could only imagine what he was saying to her. My own parents had fought like crazy when I was a kid, so in an odd way, I never thought it was strange at that point. Besides, we were heavily in development on a number of other projects, and yelling was pretty normal around the office. I'd roll calls for thirty minutes or more each night and listen to my boss screaming at nearly everybody we got on the phone.

This was exactly how I became privy to the conversation where she told the new writer to sit down with her husband and listen to his bullshit stories, butter him up and there'd be real paid assignments down the road. It was during this time I got the impression this joint family project they'd supposedly been talking about since before they got married wasn't really all that important to her.

As we came closer to getting into production on another film, it became obvious he was getting irate at being pushed to the back burner. She'd gotten a couple of agents to take a cursory look at the new script, but none were responding to it.

The marriage deteriorated rapidly after that. She'd gone on a location-scouting trip without him and he suspected infidelity. He'd gone off to Vegas for a weekend with his friends and refused to talk about what he'd done there.

One Monday she came in late. She told me she had moved out after a heated argument where he'd pushed her down to the flagstone on the back patio. She'd had enough. She had me call her lawyer about a restraining order.

Over the next few months, things got uglier. He made it clear that he was going to sue for alimony given the state of his comparatively smaller income. She hit the roof.

Her work suffered too. The film project she'd scouted fell through when the director bailed to do a bigger movie. Another project she'd been nursing since before I began working there finally died when the writer decided not to let her renew the option on it for yet another year. It was like a dark cloud parked itself over my boss. She fought back by yelling at everyone around her even more. I started to feel like hiding under my desk every time she came into the office.

The subpoena for me to appear at a deposition in the matter of the divorce came right to the office. I cried because I thought I'd have to hire a lawyer and couldn't afford one, especially on my meager salary.

For the next two weeks, my boss and her lawyer coached me on how to answer certain questions. I was terrified. My deposition was to be made under oath. More than once, my mother told me to just tell the truth as best as I could.

The morning of the deposition, I threw up.

I arrived at the office of her husband's lawyer and was escorted into a conference room. Waiting for me were my boss, her husband, their lawyers, a stenographer and a man operating a video camera. I was offered a glass of water and couldn't remember if I'd accepted it before someone set it in front of me.

The questions started. Had I ever been in a deposition before? No. Did I know how a deposition works? No.

The process was quickly described to me. It seemed the same as it did in the movies.

More questions: How long had I worked for my boss? How did I get the job? What was I hoping my job would lead to? This went on for nearly an hour before the first curveball was thrown at me.

"Did (my boss' husband) ever make any sexual advances toward you?"

I was stunned. *What*?

The lawyer repeated the question. I answered quickly "No."

This was just the beginning. They asked if my boss' husband ever used any profanity around me. If he'd ever shown me lewd pictures. If he'd ever offered me pot or other drugs. If he'd ever offered me a drink. If he'd ever yelled at me or thrown anything at me.

I answered no on all counts. I tried not to make eye contact with my boss, but could tell this had something to do with portions of the case I didn't know anything about. I wasn't sure if I'd answered incorrectly, but I did remember my mother's advice to just tell the truth.

Different aspects of my relationship with my boss' husband were being probed. Since there wasn't anything to tell, I managed one-word answers to nearly all of their questions.

And then they asked about my boss' gun.

It took me by surprise. I didn't know she had one. She never mentioned it. I was asked if I'd ever seen her take it out of her purse. I said no. I was asked if I was present on the night she pointed it at her husband—the same night she told me he'd pushed her down to the flagstone.

I answered that I hadn't been there. They asked what I'd known about the incident. I told them what she'd told me. The version I'd rehearsed with my boss a few days earlier was fresh in my mind. He was drunk. She wanted a divorce. He pushed her with both hands so hard she'd fallen onto the floor of the patio.

The lawyer for my husband's boss asked me again if I was there. Again, I told him no. He asked me if I realized my story was all hearsay. I paused and answered yes. He asked me if I was sure I'd been told he'd shoved her with both hands. If my boss' husband had put down his drink before shoving her to the ground. I was being trapped into making it sound like the story was all made up.

He asked me if I was aware that my boss had also pulled a gun on her first husband years earlier. I told him no. He asked if my boss had ever pulled a gun on me. I paused because I couldn't believe he was asking me that, but my momentary silence felt wrong in the room. It felt like I was hiding something. I answered, no, she hadn't. He asked me again if I'd ever seen my boss' gun. I emphatically told him no, but once again I felt like the way I answered made it seem like I was hiding something.

I suddenly felt very aware of every eyeball in the room on me. Even the guy operating the video camera gazed at me with suspicion in his eyes. I must have looked exactly the way I felt inside, because someone asked if I needed a break. I answered yes and bolted out of the conference room like it was on fire.

Another lawyer, a female one, found me in a stall in the ladies' room, bawling my eyes out. She asked if I was okay. I told her I didn't want to go back in the conference room. She calmly explained that I had to answer some more questions and I could come back tomorrow to do it if I didn't feel up to doing it today. The thought of going through all of this again made me even more sick. Finally, I composed myself and went back in to resume my seat.

The questions came fast and furious. How was my boss' business doing? Did she mention that she was abandoning her husband's script because of marital problems? How many out-of-town trips had she taken without him? At some point my eyes found a spot on the wall and stayed there. The questions, and my subsequent answers, became a blur. This went on for two more hours.

Finally it ended. I was released from my sworn duty in the chair of inquisition and allowed to go home. I exited the conference room and expected my boss to be there. I wanted a hug, a shoulder squeeze, something. She and her lawyer were still huddled inside, speaking in hushed whispers. I left quietly, speaking only to the receptionist who validated my parking ticket.

I drove home, numb. I couldn't even call my mother from the car since I had forgotten to charge my phone the night before. Somehow, I made it home without paying attention.

When I got back to my place, my mother had already left three messages on my machine. I called her back and spent the next hour and a half recounting what had happened. Her horror at the way I was treated triggered my own anger. As I was getting tired, my call waiting beeped. I clicked over.

It was my boss.

"You did good in there today," she told me.

I stammered a response. I thought I had talked too much.

"You told them nothing," she said. I could almost tell she'd had a drink or two. "We'll talk about it tomorrow."

When I went into the office the next morning, my boss told me the same thing. She said I did what I had to do under oath, but they'd have a tough time mining any real info from my testimony. She thanked me again. It was the last we spoke about it.

As if nothing had happened, business returned to normal immediately. By the end of the day my anxiety had left and I was feeling normal. By the end of the week, I was finally able to laugh about it with my friends.

But then the next week came, and on Friday I received my pay stub. I looked at it. I blinked and looked again.

I'd been docked by my boss. The day I'd been deposed was counted as time off without pay.

THE MANAGER, CURRENT PROGRAMMING (MCP)

If I were to tell you that my boss, the MCP, was working underneath the V.P., I would mean it in more ways than one.

She was ten years his junior, but light years ahead of him everywhere else. He had come aboard the company from a job at a fairly large cable network that had been floundering. His experience shepherding hit programming was questionable, but the big boss felt his career had been impressive enough. At first he came in all bluster and sparkle, but for most people in the office, the bloom came off that rose pretty early. He had a habit of rubbing people the wrong way, especially everyone else in the department. My boss at that time was no different. She couldn't stand him from the very first day he took over the office down the hall.

When others would disparage him behind his back for his brash behavior and the gossipy rumors he liked to throw around, she would skewer him in his absence. When he began to question the president of production's wherewithal during the middle of a particularly embarrassing pilot season, she helped fuel the fire of doubt that the big boss was failing because he had hired the wrong guy to look after the studio's interests. With all earnestness, she would often sit in her office and tell me she thought he was a poison pill.

In time, she became practically obsessed with how much of a jerk he was becoming. She would report back to me every little thing he did that bugged her. One week it would be a story about how he pulled a show's co-star aside at a table read to tell her how she should look at tapes of last season's episodes because he preferred the way she did her character then. Another week, it would be how certain writers were taking advantage of new minority hiring initiatives to make up for their lack of ability. The thing that worried me the most, was how often she would tell me that she despised him, sometimes using the invective up to three times in a sentence: "I hate, hate, hate him." That was the point I began to fear that deep down inside, she was developing a thing for him.

I'm not exactly certain when they began sleeping together. I believe it was during Upfront week (when all the networks announced their fall schedules). All I can tell you is that when they returned from New York, everything changed. I noticed it for the first time when he began dropping by her office several more times a day than was usual. Each time with a wink and a grin for me as he swept through her door like Hef at the Playboy Mansion. From my desk, I could hear her laugh at the dumb (and probably dirty) jokes he was telling her. Even her near-daily diatribes about what a lout he was had gone on the wane. Several times, I tried to get the courage to ask her what was going on, but failed to get the words out of my mouth on each occasion. The clincher came while rolling calls for her late one Friday afternoon and she asked me to dial him up at a resort in Palm Desert, and then jump off the line. As soon as he picked up I heard his lascivious-sounding greeting.

"'Bout time you called," he said. I hung up the phone, now certain she was on her way out to see him.

When her cell phone bill came in I noticed a growing pattern of calls to his cell phone—calls she didn't have me make for her. I wanted to at least say something to her in private about discretion, but feared I was treading into dangerous waters with this one.

One weekend, I was out with some friends, one of whom brought along a boyfriend who still worked at the cable net where my boss' new flame had last been employed.

"(Name withheld)," my friend's boyfriend whistled. "He had a reputation for being kind of a *Svengali*," he leaned in and told me. "Apparently he has this way of coming into an office and finding the one person he can totally manipulate to align with him. When he worked for us, he started sleeping with this guy in the legal department. That's why he isn't at (cable network name withheld) anymore."

I sat there with my jaw on the table.

"He was sleeping with some *guy?*" I asked. So totally in shock that the room began to spin around me.

"Yup," my friend's boyfriend said. "Stay away from (name withheld), that dude is the Prince of Darkness."

I went into the office on Monday very conflicted. My boss had been really great to me. I even considered her to be kind of a mentor and a role model. In short, I wanted to be her someday. In my heart, I wanted to tell her what I had heard. I'd known my friend's boyfriend for a while and considered him to be a straight-forward guy, not a bullshitter, so I had no reason to doubt his version of the story. But then again, gossip was gossip. I wanted to tell her, *sister to sister*, but after many conversations with my friends about the matter, decided it wasn't my place to do so.

Until I had more evidence.

I started with the obvious. I cleverly arranged another outing with my friend and her boyfriend, giving myself ample opportunity to grill him again. From him, I realized I knew another person who had worked in the same place my boss' beau had worked before. I had them meet me for drinks at Hama Sushi. They told me the same thing that my friend's boyfriend did. The man in question was a wolf in sheep's clothing, who apparently wasn't too particular about which side of the plate he batted from, or who got hurt in the process. I was given names, dates, places; enough evidence to convict.

And that's when things started to get funny. His stops at her door were becoming less and less frequent. The cell phone calls were tapering off. My boss, who had always been a rock emotionally, turned sullen. For nearly two weeks she would come in, lock herself in her office and order in for lunch if she didn't have an appointment. Other than things having to do with general business, she probably spoke no more than a dozen sentences to me. Finally, one afternoon I broke down and asked if everything was alright.

"You've been asking about him, haven't you?" she told me. I was stunned, totally not expecting her to say this. I wasn't about to lie. I told her I had, but didn't say why.

"Word got back to him, you know," she said. I realized my Hama Sushi rendezvous pal had sold me out. "He thinks I put you up to it."

I could see where this was going. I could see the short end of the stick coming my way. I wanted to tell her the things I heard. Sure it was unsubstantiated gossip, but I wanted it clear that anything I had done was out of concern for her feelings. I had to decide to spill the beans or keep it to myself.

I could tell she was upset. I began to open my mouth, but her words stopped me.

"None of those stories are true, you know." Her eyes were glaring at me. "It's all vicious slander spread by an old, disgruntled assistant."

I could see she believed every word of what she was saying. I wanted to believe it too, but a little voice in my head was telling me that everything I heard came from two different sources working at two different companies. Were people in this town so quick to jump on a rumor that they'd peddle a juicy one as their own? Suddenly, I realized what a fool I'd been played for. I tried apologizing, but the words were coming out wrong from my mouth.

"I called around and found you another job," my boss said. I was going to be moved to another desk, but at a different location, working for someone I'd never met before. I'd been traded for a player to be named later. She told me she had done me that solid instead of having me fired because I was good at what I do. I just had to learn not to go sticking my nose where it didn't belong.

Stung. That's how I felt as I went to my desk. I could barely comprehend how my good deed turned into this. I went down to the copy room to get a couple of empty boxes to put my stuff into. I felt as though I had let her down.

Upon my return, the V.P. was in her office talking in a hushed voice. I wanted to know what they were saying, but thought to myself that I'd done enough snooping already.

Minutes later, when he came out of her office, he looked at me on his way down the hall and winked. I never forgot that.

My new boss was nowhere as cool as my old boss. He was a screamer and a worrywart. I was working in business affairs and missed the sexy goings-on of being near the heartbeat of current programming. I read less scripts and learned to properly decipher a P & L sheet. My friends told me to look for another job if I was unhappy, but I just couldn't bring myself to do it. I think I looked at my reassignment as a kind of penance I had to pay for messing up a good thing. Rarely, if ever, did I bump into my old boss even though I looked for her in her old haunts.

Eventually though, I did find another job with another company and I found out that my old boss did get back together with the V.P. and continued a clandestine relationship for several more months before breaking up. I heard from some former colleagues in my old department that it ended badly and she was devastated, both by the heartbreak and the fact she had aligned herself with this guy on so many professional matters that she was really left holding the bag when he hung her out to dry. I had to say I felt bad for her.

About a year later, I myself had finally become a junior executive. One day, during an event at the Television Academy, I bumped into him. He smiled, shook my hand and asked how I was doing. I played it cool, but his warm, friendly manner really caught me off guard. As he put his hand on my shoulder, he told me I was going to make a great exec. I could only stare into those deep blue eyes of his and think of how handsome he really was up close.

☆ ☆ ☆ ☆ ☆

THE VERY BIG STAR (VBS)

This is a story that happened a great many years ago, but I can tell it now because my boss at the time is no longer with us. He was a VBS, and, as was his usual routine while on location, he would hook up with some local beauty for the duration of his short stay away from home. With a wink, he often told me the memories gained from bedding young ladies from around the world would be the fire that would keep him warm in his golden years. Even though those so-called "golden years" were nipping at his heels, he showed no signs of slowing down. After all, he felt it was his obligation to sample everything the world had to offer.

Our shoot south of the border had mostly centered around less-than-stellar conditions, and my boss was ready to pack up and go home. As was his way, he would take his local paramour out for one last blast before saying goodbye. Most of them wept, crying thankful tears of farewell, knowing they themselves now had their own tiny fire to warm them in their own golden years. At least this was the way my boss chose to see it.

This time, however, his lady did not take it so well. After a meal he specially had flown in from Chasen's, followed by several bottles of very expensive French wine and nearly twenty-four hours of passionate lovemaking, she took the news as some kind of betrayal. She scratched his face, bloodied his lip and nearly took his head off with a lamp she launched at his head. To say she stormed out heartbroken and angry would be a complete understatement.

My boss was no monster, and he felt really terrible about what had happened Two days later, production wrapped, and I could see it was still bothering him. Before the last take of the last scene, he whispered in my ear that he was going to need, "a sweet goodbye.."

In his parlance, "a sweet goodbye" meant he was going to give her an expensive gift. The gift of choice was almost always a Rolex engraved with both her initials and his. I don't know exactly how many "sweet goodbyes" he had bestowed in his lifetime, but I'm fairly certain the number had easily paid for his jeweler's kids' college fund. I got on the horn and ordered one up, super express. It showed up several hours later. I tipped the courier with a hundred dollar bill.

Usually, as practice, a "sweet goodbye" was never given in person, but handed over by a qualified messenger. However, not this time. After several drinks at the hotel's bar for both of us, my boss decided he would do the right thing and deliver it himself. It was getting late, and I could see his reasoning most likely included one last taste of the local honey. I wasn't about to let him go, but when he told me she had a sister, my reticence dissolved like smoke. I'd seen his local lady, and the chance to be with anyone who shared even the smallest bit of genetic makeup as her was worth the risk we were about to take. My boss called her from the bar and told her we were coming over.

After another drink, we stumbled to the curb and hailed a cab. My boss had been to her place once and claimed he could find it again in any state of inebriation. I looked out the window with trepidation at the mean streets of a city that looked a lot worse after midnight.

The cab dropped us off in front of an apartment building, and right away I could feel things had gone badly even before my boss mumbled we were on the wrong street. To my chagrin, I looked up to see the cab had disappear into the darkness. We were in a neighborhood that had never even heard of streetlights.

My inclination was to run like hell until I found a pay phone so I could wake up someone from the crew back at the hotel. My boss was nonplussed. He claimed his intuition told him we were close. We were only four blocks off target. He told me to trust him.

By the time we turned the corner, I sobered up immensely. For my boss, this had become yet another grand adventure he often bragged would become a chapter in his eventual autobiography. This story however, would not have a happy ending for either of us.

Halfway down the second block, I heard the footstep from behind. A man emerged from a darkened doorway we had just passed. My blood froze. Even in the dim moonlight, there was no mistaking the gun he was holding on us.

In guttural Spanish, he told us to empty our pockets and give him our watches. I had a couple hundred dollars, about a thousand pesos, and a Timex. My boss always carried a roll of at least five grand in cash, and didn't wear a watch. In his pocket, however, was the jeweled Rolex that had come down from Beverly Hills. The gunman took it from my boss, not even bothering to glance at what was inside the box. As he waved his pistol around nervously, I was literally shaking in my shoes. The effects of several shots of Patron I had imbibed earlier had definitely worn off. My boss kept quiet.

The gunman looked around. The street was dark and deserted. "Get on your knees," he said. He repeated it in a more serious tone.

I can't say my life flashed before my eyes, but I was pretty certain the gunman was going to put a bullet into my head. I was beyond scared. I was terrified to the point of complete and total paralysis.

"I can get you more money," my boss pleaded.

"Shut up," the gunman hissed in Spanish. He began to unbuckle his pants. With a dirty hand, he pulled out his small stiff prick and stuck it in my boss' face.

"Now you're going to suck my dick," he said. To make his point he pressed the barrel of the gun against my boss' forehead.

As the gunman's dick disappeared beyond my boss' lips, I turned away and closed my eyes. I wanted to cry, but to be perfectly honest, I was afraid if I made a noise the gunman would turn and make me suck him off, too.

I'm not so sure how much time passed, but it felt like forever and with each passing second, I prayed someone would come to our rescue. No such luck. Finally, the gunman finished up his business with a low, sharp grunt. He pulled his dripping cock back into his pants and ran down the street into the darkness.

My boss grabbed me with both hands, very much shaken. "He came in my mouth," he grimaced.

"Let's get out of here," I said. Truthfully, I was afraid our attacker would come back with some friends. My boss began down the street in a hurry. As we turned another corner, I was hoping we'd find a police station or a pay phone. Instead it was another row of slums.

"I recognize this street. Her place is right up here," he said. I couldn't believe it. He was still looking for the apartment of his local lady. Though given our circumstances, I wasn't sure at the time if we really had too many options. Any port in a storm, they say. It would turn out to be a really bad idea.

As we approached the building, we could see four guys lingering by the front of the building, waiting for something. Waiting for us.

Before we made it halfway down the block, they stepped in front of our path. From a window I could see someone watching. It was my boss' local lady. Once she knew we were coming, she had her two brothers and a couple of guys from his street gang wait for us with a message. She wanted my boss to rot in hell. We never got a chance to explain because her brothers and their two buddies proceeded to kick the living shit out of us. I remember fists pummeling my face before blacking out entirely. At some point while I was unconscious, my boss was able to find someone to drive us back to the hotel. My jaw had been dislocated. One of my eyes was swollen shut. My boss, even at his age, managed to hold them off of him for a brief period before taking a very severe beating.

We packed and left immediately. My boss arranged for a private car to take us all the way back to Los Angeles. We left without saying goodbye to anyone. My boss assured me that anyone who worked at the hotel who saw our condition would chalk it up to his legendary reputation for drinking, whoring and fighting. We traveled the rest of the way home in complete silence.

He had the car take me to the hospital and paid for all of my medical bills. As far as I know, he never told anybody about what happened that night. After a couple of days at home with his family, he took a solitary trip to the south of France for three weeks, perhaps in an attempt to reassemble the bits of sanity he had left or perhaps to visit his local lady there. I never asked.

THE YOUNG FILM MAKER (YFM)

My boss got his big break after graduating from UCLA when he sold the screenplay he'd penned as his thesis project for a cool half-million bucks.

By the time he was twenty-three, he'd already been hired to write a pair of scripts for Warners and had sold a very big pitch to Fox that had made the front page of Variety. He was considered to be a young genius; one of the new generation that would shape the future of Hollywood.

When I was twenty-three, I was waiting tables on a cruise ship because I'd run out of money for school. That continued for a year until I watched a girl I worked with die from a heroin overdose. After that, I decided to go back and finish my Film School degree.

Two days shy of my twenty-seventh birthday, a professor of mine called to let me know he was recommending me to be the assistant to a hot new young filmmaker. When he said "young," I had no idea he meant someone four years younger than myself.

At first it was kind of strange. Not only was my new boss younger than me, but because I clock in at six-foot three-inches, he was easily half a foot shorter. During the day, he'd spend countless hours playing Xbox and smoking weed with some other UCLA Film School Mafia buddies of his while they carried on an endless discourse about whatever pop cultural bullshit anybody dared bring up. After I clocked out at six, my boss retreated to his second bedroom-turned-office to pound out his latest work until the wee hours of the morning.

Most mornings, I'd arrive at his townhouse in the Hollywood Hills at noon since he rarely, if ever, woke before eleven. He'd given me a key, so I'd let myself in to find him in his usual seat at the kitchen counter eating Corn Pops and reading the L.A. Times. After checking for phone messages, I'd go about the task of dealing with the day's chores. If there were script pages to be faxed or messengered out, I took care of it. If dry cleaning needed to be dropped off or picked up, I ran out and handled it. Once a week, I would arrange for groceries to be delivered to his place during the hours I was working. I kept my boss' life in order six hours a day for a grand wage of four hundred bucks a week.

Around two or three in the afternoon, my boss' little entourage would start showing up and my job at this point would often turn into food gopher since I would be sent out to make a Starbucks run for my boss' little gang. One time, after I made the mistake of mentioning to my boss that I knew how to operate a cappuccino machine, he made me order a fifteen hundred dollar Pasquini Livia espresso maker for his already cramped kitchen. Soon, I became the barista to the entire entourage. The novelty of the machine escaped nobody since they would command cup after cup of rich dark espresso, which I would have to make. After the first three or so, something about the combination of loads of caffeine, the testosterone-filled rush of violent video games and the occasional joint would turn the mood in the place into something akin to a rowdy frat house. One day, one of my boss' friends, the balding guy who always wore the Paramount Pictures baseball cap, commanded to me in a spot-on Jack Nicholson impression: "Where's my fucking latte?"

For some reason, that busted the room into hysterics. As he repeated it, my boss was doubled over in laughter.

And from that day on, it stuck. Anytime someone wanted me to make them a cup of joe with the fancy doohickey in the kitchen, it was my job to respond to: "Where's my fucking latte?"

The house's new catch phrase quickly ingrained itself into everyday use to the point where my boss would shout it out to me when I first arrived as his way of saying he'd like me to make him a cup of something dark and sweet. After all, I was the only one who knew how to operate the damn thing.

Just as one of my boss' movies was ramping up to go into production, he began seeing, or more accurately in his parlance, *banging* one of the actresses he'd met at a party. One morning, I was arriving just as she was leaving, having obviously spent the night. My boss pulled me aside, first to tell me what a great piece of ass she was, and second, to have me show him how to use the espresso machine lurking on the kitchen counter. Apparently, his new bedmate had wanted a post-coital jolt of java, and he'd felt dumb standing there in front of the thing not even knowing how to use it.

I'd never been the type to be considered a patient teacher, but I did my best to run through the basic steps of using the Pasquini Livia. My boss took notes, often looking down and writing as I showed him one step or another. I told him that my secret in steaming the milk was to keep it ice cold in a metal pitcher, and then when steaming it, use a thermometer to make sure it reached one hundred forty degrees Fahrenheit. When I asked him if he'd gotten it down, he told me it was no problem.

Two days later, after the actress had again stayed the night, he met me at the door wearing a bathrobe, his hand in a bandage.

"You never said not to hold the milk pitcher by the bottom," he blurted. I could tell he considered the burn he'd gotten to be my fault. He showed me the welt on his hand from the scalding hot milk he'd spilled on himself. It was ugly.

When I entered the kitchen, I found the Pasquini Livia face down on the floor.

"I got a little angry," my boss said. He turned away and went up to his bedroom, which was obviously my cue to clean up this mess. As I picked up the small metal pitcher, I wondered why it never occurred to my young genius boss to use the handle someone had bothered to weld onto the side.

My boss yelled out my name. I went upstairs to see what was going on. I found him, half-dressed, trying in vain to button the front of a shirt with his non-dominant left hand.

"Can you help me with this?" he asked. I stood in the doorway. I'd never been allowed into his bedroom before.

The place looked like a stereotypical bachelor lived here. The black sheets and black bedspread were in disarray and a nearly empty bottle of Skyy Vodka sat next to the alarm clock, along with an open box of condoms.

As I buttoned up my boss' shirt, I could feel his embarrassment. At first I thought it was because of what I was doing, but then caught his eyes looking at something on the floor. Involuntarily, I snuck a peek.

Sitting in a heap by the bed was a strap-on dildo in a harness.

His eyes caught mine. Having played a lot of poker during my cruise ship years, I kept my face straight and unemotional. My boss could apparently see something else in my eyes.

"Oh come on, like you never walked on the wild side," he said with a hint of something uncomfortable in his voice.

If you mean having some chick stuff a big rubber dong up my butt, then no, I thought.

"Sure," I lied. My sex life had been mostly plain vanilla to the extent my last serious girlfriend had dubbed me the "missionary man."

"Something about the way it feels having that thing inside of me makes me come so much harder," he said as straight out as if he were raving instead about his cell phone or the anti-lock brakes on his Yukon.

This was the point where I was becoming very uncomfortable being in the room. Having a discussion with my boss about him getting ham-slammed with chunk of stiff latex was not in my job description. I could tell from his uncomfortable smile that he knew we'd crossed some kind of line into an area best not to ventured into.

"I'm going to finish cleaning up in the kitchen," I told him. Though I wanted to run from the room as if I was on fire, I managed to calmly walk out.

My boss stayed upstairs for a couple of hours, presumably cleaning up and possibly hiding from me. I sat at the kitchen table, paying a stack of his bills, keeping my head down.

Around the usual time, the posse showed up as always and my boss came down and acted as though nothing strange had happened between us. His friends were bummed at the loss of the Pasquini Livia, and upon the first command of "Where's my fucking latte?" I got in my car and wheeled down to Starbucks like in the old days. Halfway down the hill, I was at a light when absentmindedly, I said to myself, "Where's my fucking dildo?" and began laughing so hard tears were rolling down my cheeks.

THE STUDIO EXECUTIVE (SEX)

I thought I was the envy of my peers when I got hired to be the assistant to the single prettiest SEX on the lot. As a young guy, I'd look at her short skirts and the bit of cleavage she would show, and my mind would drift to fantasies of having to work late and the forbidden tryst with the boss on her desk after everyone else had gone home. To make it worse, she was single and hardly ever dated because she didn't have the time for a relationship.

One day, she was on the phone and I came into her office with a messenger package that had just been delivered. I could see that she had one hand between her knees, fiddling with something. She looked up at me and hurriedly shooed me out of her office. I went back to my desk, wondering what she was doing in there.

About one minute later, she called me to come back in. Still on the phone, she handed me her trash basket and told me to go dump this. I took it, and as I'm carrying it down the hallway, I noticed the bloody Kleenex poking out from inside. Upon closer inspection, to my horror, there was a used tampon rolled up in the tissue. She had been so busy talking on this important conference call that she couldn't even take a break to go change it in the bathroom.

THE TV DIRECTOR (TVD)

The trip to Maui was something my boss the TVD had been planning for hiatus. When it came, I was glad he was going to be away for a couple of weeks. Personally, I needed the break from being around him.

The first few days were complete bliss. The phone never rang, and I had a chance to finally catch up on all the tape-logging and follow-up stuff that had been on the back-burner. I spent a whole Thursday lazily filling out some Guild forms he'd forgotten about, while I drank his expensive coffee. I scribbled my version of his signature on them, then took a nice long walk to the post office, enjoying being outside for a change. By the weekend I felt relaxed for the first time in weeks.

Saturday night, I'd made plans to meet up with some friends and go club-hopping. I needed it. I was showered and dressed and putting on my shoes when my phone rang.

It was my boss.

"I locked my keys in the car," he said.

I groaned. I was about to tell him to call AAA when I realized he only had the roadside protection that came with his BMW. It would be useless with a rental car. I wasn't sure what I'd be able to do to help him.

"The car's running, too," he said. He and his girlfriend had been in such a rush to get to a luau that he'd parked the car and left it running in the parking lot. I suspected there'd been some alcohol in the equation somewhere as well.

"I need you to look up the number of the rental car company and call me back." He hung up before I could protest.

I was pissed but not surprised. I went to my computer to get the info he wanted. Of course my cable modem chose that moment to slow to a molasses-like crawl. I checked my watch ten times in five minutes.

Finally, I called him back with the number. He reacted like I was an idiot.

"I wanted you to call them," he said. "That's what I told you."

That's not what I had heard, but I figured I'd just do it. He was annoyed, and I was going to be late if I argued the point.

I hung up with him and dialed the car rental company on the island. As the phone rang on the other end, I realized I'd forgotten an important piece of information.

I called my boss back.

"Where are you?" I asked.

"Old Lahaina Luau," he said.

I hung up again and called the rental car company. On the island it was after eight p.m. The phone rang a dozen times before someone picked it up. I explained the situation. They told me they could send someone out, but Lahaina was forty minutes away and it might take their driver over an hour since he was out on another call. I told them to go ahead and send the guy as soon as possible.

I called my boss back.

"An hour?" he said. I wanted to remind him that was the price he'd have to pay for being so dumb to begin with.

"Call a tow truck," he said. "Someone local. I don't care, I'll pay for it."

I hung up again and groaned. I called the rental car company and cancelled their driver. Then I went back to my computer and spent another five excruciatingly slow minutes looking up tow trucks in Lahaina. While I waited for my glacier-slow Internet connection to spit out some names, I called my friends to tell them I was running behind schedule.

I got three numbers and called them all. They told me that they wouldn't be able to legally open the car door. They could only tow it. I was told I'd have to call a locksmith. I got a couple of numbers. I hung up, amazed at how polite all the native Hawaiians had been.

The first locksmith I called said he could do it, for a hundred bucks cash. I told him I'd have to call him back.

I called my boss.

"I'm not paying a hundred bucks!" he said. "Call someone else."

I went back to my computer and checked my watch. An hour earlier I was moments from the first fun Saturday night I'd had in weeks. I opened a beer I'd had in my fridge and waited for my computer.

As I was calling another locksmith, my call-waiting beeped. It was my boss. He told me to just call the first locksmith. He'd pay the hundred bucks.

I hung up and imagined his girlfriend had finally talked some sense into him. I called back the first locksmith and panicked when I got an answering machine. He picked up when I started leaving a message. He said he'd be there in twenty minutes. He asked what kind of car it was.

I called my boss again.

"A Mustang," he said. "White."

I wanted to ask him if it was a convertible, but decided not to. I was getting punchy. I told him the guy said twenty minutes. He told me to tell the guy to hurry.

When I called the locksmith back, he changed his estimate to thirty minutes. I said I had told my boss twenty. The locksmith said he'd get there as soon as he could.

I looked at my watch. If I hadn't called off the guy from the rental car place, he'd probably already be there.

I grabbed my car keys. I was finally going to go out. As I got into my car, I called my boss back with what I was hoping would be a final update.

"Stay close until this guy shows up, just in case I need you to call someone else."

I turned my car off and went back inside. I could wait a little longer.

Twenty minutes later, I called my boss. I was antsy and wanted to know if I could leave. He said the locksmith hadn't showed up. He wanted me to call the guy and tell him to hurry up.

I called the locksmith and got his machine. On the outgoing message I realized he'd left a cell phone number. I called it. The locksmith told me he was on his way.

I called my boss back. He wanted a specific estimate of how much longer he'd have to wait.

I called the locksmith back. He politely told me five minutes.

I called my boss. He told me I had to call the locksmith back and let him know he wasn't parked at the Luau, but in the auxiliary lot across the street behind the Long's Drugs.

I called the locksmith and told him. He said he'd be there in five minutes. I realized that's what he said five minutes ago.

I watched the clock. Six minutes later, my boss called me. The locksmith still wasn't there. He told me to call this guy and chew him a new one.

I wasn't in the mood for it. Especially given how nice the guy had been on the phone.

"Just do it!" my boss said. He was truly annoyed.

I called the locksmith back. He said he was just turning down Front Street now. He was a block away.

I called my boss back to tell him the good news. Ten seconds into the conversation, I heard the locksmith pull up. He was very apologetic about taking so long to get there. He told my boss I'd called him three times to make sure he knew where to find the car.

I could hear my boss put on his "charismatic snake-charmer voice." Through the earpiece I heard him tell the locksmith, "I apologize for the rudeness of my assistant."

THE PRODUCTION COMPANY VICE PRESIDENT (PCVP)

There is no crazier time in television than pilot season. Our company had gone into selling mode the previous fall with five scripts everyone was excited about. Among them was a one-hour created by a guy who'd penned a huge summer movie a couple of years back. This was my boss', the PCVP's, pet project. Through an agent that repped our company, we were secretly getting slipped copies of other people's pilot scripts. Most of them were complete drek. The hush-hush talk around the office was that if lightning struck and we scored big and got all, or at least four of our scripts picked up for pilot commitments, we'd have to expand and bring on more people. For me that possibly meant getting kicked up from the assistant desk I'd manned for two years. Our scripts went to the networks and I kept my fingers crossed. I'd been chomping at the bit for a shot.

I could tell there was going to be trouble when my boss spent a half hour on a conference call, screaming at our go-to guy at (network name deleted). The newly-appointed head of drama development wasn't on board with what our semi-famous screenwriter had done. They had notes and wanted changes. One of them, for reasons nobody could understand, involved changing the lead's human best friend into a dog whose thoughts only the audience could hear. They even envisioned a romantic relationship between the mutt and a poodle that lived next door. My boss nearly had an embolism. He thought they were nuts.

When the dust settled, only two of our projects were going to pilot; one drama and one sitcom. Neither of them was my boss' pet project. We licked our wounds and went forward. My boss hid his disappointment, but I could see it in his face.

Casting went smoothly and, with the help of the network, we lined up a fairly well-known movie helmer to direct the pilot. Production was slated to start the first week of February. My boss, however, was still a bit sore and griped to me quite a bit that he thought the drama (network name deleted) was picking up was nowhere near as good as his pet project. I saw my opportunity and asked to shadow him as much as possible during production. I was hoping he'd see this as a chance to let someone else pay attention to this turd so he didn't have to. He told me it would be a great idea.

We booked a soundstage at (studio name deleted) to shoot for eight days. I'd begun my entertainment "career" there giving back lot tours so I was pretty psyched to go back as part of a production. I felt like it was just a matter of time before I was bumped up to executive.

I strolled onto the stage as they were prepping to shoot the very first scene. I'd been there two days before while they were still putting up the set, and my eyes popped at the job they'd done. I'd been to plenty of TV show locations before, but this was by far the most amazing. The attention to detail was incredible. I had a good feeling about how much of the pilot's two million dollar budget was being used for sets and I could see we were really getting our money's worth on screen. As I was marveling over some of the antique furnishings, my cell phone rang; it was my boss, his manicure was running late. He told me to hold down the fort until he got there. I told him it would be no problem.

Two days in, and things were moving along mostly on schedule and on budget. On day three, one of the supporting actresses showed up to film her first scenes. I'd seen her in a couple of small TV roles before, and had always been smitten.

I'd been looking forward to meeting her ever since I found out she'd been cast as one of the female lead's sassy friends. I covertly peeked in on her while she was in the make-up trailer and watched from behind the line while she shot her first couple of scenes. It wasn't until later when she went out for a smoke that I dared introduce myself.

She was outside of the stage puffing on a cigarette, and I went out to bum a smoke off her. I told her who I was and shook her hand. She had these two tiny three-month old teacup yorkies and we watched them play and yip at each other while making idle chit-chat. She smiled at me when she finished her cigarette, picked up her dogs and went back inside. I thought about that smile all day.

The next day we repeated the same routine. The two of us smoking and watching her dogs play. This time I brought my own cigarettes that I'd picked up at a gas station on the way in. A friend of mine told me the way to get an actress to like you is to ask her a lot of questions about herself. I tried it and it worked like a charm. From the things she was saying, I was able to intimate that she didn't have a boyfriend.

That afternoon, my boss got into a screaming match with the director. My boss hadn't been too happy with the performances the helmer was getting from the female lead. He thought she seemed to be more objectified than anyone was going to be comfortable with. The director spouted on about her "visual arc" and that my boss needed to trust him. That, and some last-minute, and unsolicited, changes the male lead was thinking for the script led to a long lunch break. Over at the craft services table, I asked my new favorite actress if she wanted to see something pretty cool.

One of the things I discovered during my tenure as tour guide was roof access to the soundstages on the lot. Even though we were in one of the smaller buildings, the view was pretty cool. I started talking about the history of the lot, pointing out the area of Culver City where they'd shot parts of *Gone with the Wind* and the soundstage where *Wizard of Oz* had been filmed. I pointed out where Elvis had shot *Jailhouse Rock,* and to where Mickey Rooney had done some of his

Andy Hardy movies. Having done this whole routine a million times, I knew how to sell it and she ate it up with a spoon, even though she seemed to be afraid to venture more than fifteen feet from the edge. Her two little dogs loved it, too. They wasted no time crapping all over the place.

The next to last day of shooting, she sidled up to me between takes and asked me to take her up to the roof again. She had brought a camera and wanted to take some pictures to send back to her parents. I wasted no time telling her it would be my pleasure. My boss had been eyeballing how I'd been ogling her for the past week. Half-jokingly, he told me to make sure nothing stupid happened until at least they wrapped production. With a lot riding on making this pilot shine, I could see he was feeling the pressure.

Later that afternoon, I took the actress up to the roof. This time I even carried one of her dogs. She'd put bows in their fur. As soon as they got to the roof, they began crapping all over and chasing each other around the moment we put them down. The actress took out her digital camera and snapped a half dozen pictures while I talked more about the lot's history and bided my time. Because of the rapport we'd developed during the shoot, I felt confident enough to ask her out.

Suddenly, she began yelling at her dogs. They were chasing each other toward the edge of the roof. I exploded from the spot where I was standing, but I never had a chance. The first dog ran right off of the roof and the second one, fully on the chase, followed right after it.

I made it to the edge, cautiously peeking over, my heart pounding. Both dogs lay fifty feet below on the asphalt, definitely not part of this mortal realm anymore. I thought I even saw one of them twitching, but I turned away. The actress was screaming hysterically.

Down on the ground, a small crowd had gathered. The actress had taken one look and ran back to her dressing room. My boss gave me dirty looks as we watched someone pick up the dogs and put them into a garbage bag. I explained what happened to my boss and the director who had finally come out to see what the ruckus was all about. My boss looked at me and shook his head. He headed toward the dressing rooms to do damage control.

The director looked at me and let out a long exhale. "Actresses," he huffed before heading back inside the soundstage.

ABOUT THE AUTHOR

Mark Yoshimoto Nemcoff is a bestselling and award-winning author who has been known to occasionally moonlight as a voice-over artist and independent journalist. He is a former Sirius Satellite Radio drive time show and T.V. host that has been featured by Playboy Magazine and Access Hollywood. He is the writer behind Kindle bestsellers "The Death of Osama Bin Laden" and "Where's My F***ing Latte?", an insiders look at the world of Hollywood celebrity assistants that was not only featured on Access Hollywood, but has spent over four years straight at the top of Amazon's top-selling chart in the categories of "Television" and "Movies."

Mark can be reached at: MYN@WordSushi.com

Twitter.com/MYN
Facebook.com/MYNBooks

If you enjoyed this book, please tell your friends.
-MYN

ALSO BY MARK YOSHIMOTO NEMCOFF:

NON-FICTION:

Fatal Sunset: Deadly Vacations

Admit You Hate Yourself

Pissed Off: Is Better Than Being Pissed On...

The Killing of Osama Bin Laden: How the Mission to Hunt Down a
Terrorist Mastermind was Accomplished

Go Forth and Kick Some Ass (Be the Hero of Your Own Life Story)

Where's My F*cking Latte? (And Other Stories About Being an
Assistant in Hollywood)

FICTION:

INFINITY

Transistor Rodeo

Shadow Falls: Angel of Death

Killing My Boss

Shadow Falls: Badlands

Diary of a Madman

Number One with a Bullet

The Art of Surfacing

The Doomsday Club

CPSIA information can be obtained at www.ICGtesting.com
Printed in the USA
LVOW08s1010261014

410554LV00001B/56/P